THE RED SHOES

by

Hans J. Schmidt

The Dramatic Publishing Company
Woodstock, Illinois •London, England •Melbourne, Australia

*** NOTICE ***

ISBN 0-87129-042-1

THE RED SHOES

A Play in Three Acts
For 14-23 Actors

CHARACTERS

Nine children—9 to 14 years of age

INGE	THORA	KRISTINE
HANS	ALICE	KIRSTEN
NILS	MARTA	OLUF

THE OLD SOLDIER .... who has a red beard
THE SHOEMAKER .... a good-natured but shrewd peasant woman who peddles shoes from a cart
KAREN .... a waif who has no shoes, as old as the oldest of the children
*THOMAS .... Footman to the Princess
*THE PRINCESS .... as old as Karen, who wants to be just a girl, but is already a Princess by birth and breeding
*LADY IN WAITING .... to the Princess
GRANDMOTHER NISSEN .... almost blind
NURSE .... to Grandmother Nissen
*FRU NIELSEN ..... Inge's mother, and sharp of tongue
*FRU SORENSEN .... Thora's mother
*RODHOLM .... a villager
*THE EXECUTIONER
*AN ANGEL
*ANOTHER ANGEL

*May be doubled, as they appear in only one act.

ACT ONE

The courtyard in front of a village church in Denmark. An early afternoon in summer.

ACT TWO

The same, an early Sunday morning, several days later.

ACT THREE

The same, early evening of the following Sunday.

FLOOR PLAN OF SETTING

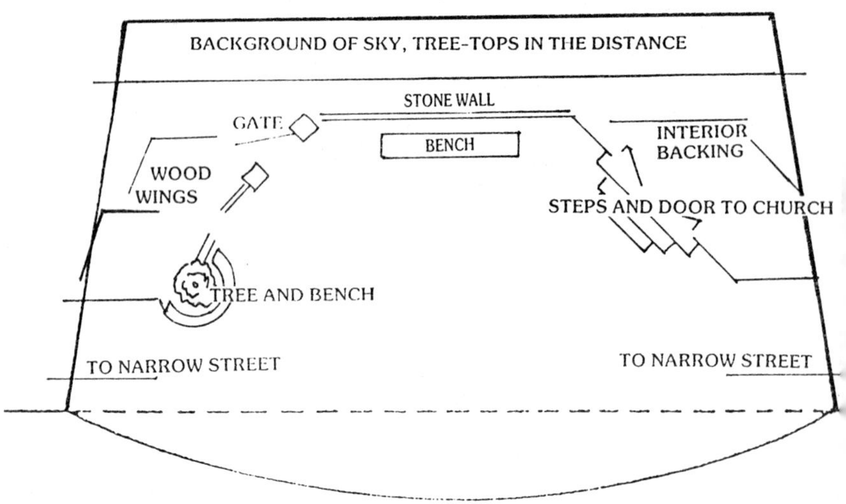

ACT ONE

As the curtain opens, we see the nine CHILDREN playing in the church courtyard. THREE of the GIRLS are on the church steps, playing jacks. The OTHER THREE GIRLS are playing hopscotch, C. NILS and OLUF are idling on the bench under the tree. HANS is sitting on the wall to the Right of the gate.

INGE *(tossing the pebble)*. There! I made it at last!
THORA. You've caught up with me now.
KRISTINE. I'm still on my threes.
THORA *(as INGE hops)*. You stepped on a line!
INGE. I did not!
THORA. You did, too! Didn't she step on a line?
INGE. You weren't looking, were you, Kristine?
HANS. I saw her. She stepped on a line, all right.
INGE *(to HANS)*. You just keep out of this!
HANS. I can see from up here!
INGE. Oh, you...! *(She rushes toward HANS who quickly slips off the fence and evades her.)*
HANS *(teasing her)*. Yah, yah, yah!
INGE. I'll get you, Hans, if it's the last thing I do! *(INGE chases HANS around the courtyard. HANS dodges skillfully. The OTHER CHILDREN watch, amused, but not too interested in the squabble.)*
HANS. Come and get me, come and get me! *(He is at the bench C. As INGE rushes toward him, he quickly steps*

up the bench and to the wall, where he walks tightrope fashion.)

INGE. Hans, get off that wall. You'll fall down the hill!

HANS. Why don't you chase me.

INGE. Not up there I won't.

HANS. See, I'm like a tightrope walker in the circus. *(He walks the wall.)*

INGE *(covering her eyes)*. I can't look!

KRISTINE. Oooooh, how can you stand it up there.

ALICE. You'll fall down the hill!

KIRSTEN. Come on down, Hans!

NILS *(to OLUF)*. How they squeal. *(To GIRLS.)* What are you girls scared of?

THORA. That's a steep hill, if he falls.

HANS *(looking behind him, as though down the hill, in mock terror)*. Ooooh, that is a steep hill. *(He cuts some fancy steps.)* Eeeeeh! Help me, I'm falling! *(He flails his arms as though trying to gain his balance, and jumps off the wall into the courtyard.)*

INGE. I could just...Oh! *(She stamps her foot in exasperation.)*

HANS *(grinning)*. Well, I didn't fall. It's nice up there. Think I'll be a tightrope walker when I grow up.

INGE. Then save your tightrope walking until you *are* grown up. *(She flounces away from him. HANS shrugs his shoulders and rejoins the BOYS, enjoying his escapade. The GIRLS return to their games.)*

THORA. It's my turn now.

INGE. I don't want to play any more. It's too hot.

THORA. You don't want to play just because you stepped on a line. I know you. Come on, Kristine.

KRISTINE. I don't want to play any more either. I never get past the threes, anyway.

THORA. All right, I'll play by myself. *(She tosses the pebble. HANS darts out and snatches the pebble. He raises his arm as though to throw it.)* Give me that pebble! *(She chases him.)*

INGE. We'll get you this time.

KRISTINE. Come on.

(The GIRLS join in chasing HANS, and he is hard-put to keep from being caught. He finds the wall well protected, and can't jump up. In the melee, the OLD SOLDIER appears at the gate.)

HANS. Help me, Nils, help me!

NILS. The gate, the gate! Run out the gate! *(HANS makes a break for the gate, and almost runs into the OLD SOLDIER. ALL stop their running to look at him.)*

SOLDIER. Good afternoon. So this is what I find at the top of the hill. Nine children running around.

THORA. He stole our hopscotch pebble.

SOLDIER. *Stole* it?

HANS. Oh, I was just teasing. Here. *(He tosses the stone to THORA.)*

SOLDIER. Do you mind if I come in? *(He makes his way to the bench under the tree.)* It's very pleasant and cool up here. *(He takes off his knapsack and sits.)* There. Now don't let me stop you from whatever you were doing.

NILS. Oh, we weren't doing anything. Just sitting around.

SOLDIER. Oh. *(He looks about him.)* Well, as I said... *(He discovers the church and rises suddenly.)* A church! I didn't know there was a church here!

KRISTINE. Didn't you see it coming along the road?

SOLDIER *(almost distastefully)*. Well, to tell you the truth, I don't usually go around looking for churches. *(He walks to the wall C and looks out over the countryside.)* Isn't there a village here?

MARTA. The village is that way. *(She indicates off DL.)* Most of it, anyway.

KIRSTEN. The hill cuts the village in two.

SOLDIER *(looking off L, then crossing to R)*. I see. And the road yonder? *(Indicating UL, off.)*

INGE. The road goes to Copenhagen.

SOLDIER *(with sudden interest)*. Copenhagen, eh? *(He looks out over the road and speaks thoughtfully to himself.)* So I was traveling the road to Copenhagen, where the Princess lives. *(He resumes his questioning and points off C.)* What's over that way?

OLUF *(indicating)*. Those are all farms.

KRISTINE *(pointing off UR)*. The woods and forests are that way.

SOLDIER. And beyond that?

OLUF. My father says that beyond the forests is the lonely place where the executioner lives.

SOLDIER. Ah! The executioner!

ALICE. What's an executioner?

SOLDIER. You don't know what an executioner is? *(He peers at the CHILDREN.)*

HANS. *I* know what he is. He chops people's heads off.

SOLDIER. Yes, he does.

ALICE. What does he do that for?

SOLDIER *(speaking very matter-of-factly)*. When people have done things they should not have done, they are punished. Some things are punished by death. So we have to have someone to...*(He makes a chopping motion on his neck.)* We call him the executioner.

NILS. I wouldn't want that kind of a job when I grow up.

THORA. Neither would I.

SOLDIER *(becoming more animated)*. Of course you wouldn't. If you were the executioner, you would have to live out there someplace, all alone. People fear him. He is dressed all in black—a black robe, a black hood, and a black mask over his eyes.

KRISTINE *(shuddering)*. Ohhhh!

SOLDIER. You would know him, if you ever met him, carrying his big axe. And you would shrink away from him, as all people do, for no one wants to be his friend. Indeed, the executioner cannot be your friend until you have nothing left to live for.

INGE. Do you know him?

SOLDIER *(recovering himself)*. In a manner of speaking, I know him, yes.

HANS. Have you seen his house?

SOLDIER. I have never seen his house. I have not traveled there.

NILS. You look as though you have traveled quite a bit.

SOLDIER. Why do you think so?

NILS. Your shoes look pretty worn.

SOLDIER. Aye, they are. I have traveled a lot.

INGE. Why?

SOLDIER. Why have I traveled? Because I am an old soldier.

HANS *(impressed)*. An old soldier! Then you have been in many battles!

SOLDIER. I have seen many a battle.

MARTA. What do you do now?

SOLDIER. Just travel. One day here, the next day there.

KRISTINE. Don't you do any work?

SOLDIER. Work? You don't see the likes of me working! Not I!

HANS. You never work? How do you get the money to buy food and clothes, and a place to sleep?

SOLDIER. That, young man, is none of your business. *(For just a moment, his voice becomes hard. Then speaking easily.)* But I'll let you in on a little secret. Everything I need is in that knapsack. Everything.

SHOEMAKER *(heard off L, chanting her wares)*. Get your shoes, get your shoes. Shoes for feet both big and small. Get your shoes, get your shoes. Shoes that hardly wear at all. *(See Production Notes for chant.)*

SOLDIER. Who is that?

KRISTINE. That is the shoe peddler.

SOLDIER. Shoe peddler, eh? *(He shows great interest and goes to the Left entrance, peering off.)* Will she come by this way?

INGE. She will if she's going to that part of the village. *(Indicating Right.)*

SOLDIER. Does she *make* shoes?

THORA. She made mine.

MARTA. And mine.

OLUF. Mine, too.

SOLDIER *(inspecting the CHILDREN's shoes)*. I see. *(After a moment's thought.)* Now you asked me a moment ago what I do for a living. I will show you *one* of the things I do for a living, if you will dance a dance for the shoemaker.

INGE. What do you mean?

SOLDIER. Just this. See? *(He has taken a musician's pipe —see Production Notes—out of his knapsack.)* I'll play you a tune if you will dance—and it won't cost you anything. *(CHILDREN exclaim their pleasure, ad lib.)* Couple up, then, couple up for the shoemaker's dance!

(The CHILDREN dance "The Shoemaker's Dance" while the OLD SOLDIER plays his pipe—see Production Notes. Presently, the SHOEMAKER enters L, pushing her shoe cart. We can see that her cart contains only work-day shoes, black in color. She has obviously come because she heard the music, and she is delighted. She dances a few steps clumsily as the dance comes to a close.)

SHOEMAKER. Eh, you play a pretty tune there, Old Soldier, if I may say so.

SOLDIER. You may say so, for I know it.

SHOEMAKER. And being the shoemaker in this countryside, I make a piper such as you most welcome.

SOLDIER. I thank you, indeed, but why a special welcome to me?

SHOEMAKER *(slyly)*. Surely if it weren't for walking and dancing, shoes would never wear out. And the more you make the children dance, the more shoes I will sell!

SOLDIER. That's the trouble with you shoemakers. You make shoes that always wear out.

SHOEMAKER. But of course! All shoes wear out!

SOLDIER. I daresay you made the shoes these children wear. Show her how your shoes are wearing out.

NILS. Mine are getting holes in them.

ALICE. So are mine.

KRISTINE. Mine are just scuffed a bit.

SHOEMAKER. Of course, of course, you silly children. You can't expect shoes to last forever.

SOLDIER. Good shoes, Dame Shoemaker, should not wear out. Should they, children.

OLUF. You are joking.

INGE. Whoever heard of shoes that never wear out!

SOLDIER. You have not heard of everything that is under the sun, have you?

SHOEMAKER *(challenging him)*. All right, old man, when and where have you met up with a pair of shoes that did not wear out?

SOLDIER *(shrugging)*. I haven't. *(Intently, as though fired by a burning ambition.)* But I have not yet finished my travels. And some day, perhaps before this day becomes yesterday, you may see dancing shoes that will not wear out.

SHOEMAKER *(lightly)*. You would have to be the one to make them, then, for I know I couldn't.

SOLDIER. I make a pair of shoes? I don't make anything. I'm an old soldier. *(With meaning.)* But you—you are a shoemaker...

SHOEMAKER. But not a shoemaker who can make shoes that last forever.

SOLDIER. Have you ever tried?

SHOEMAKER *(taken aback)*. Tried?

SOLDIER. Oh, I know you are thinking that I am—*(He taps his head.)* But *suppose* you *could* make such a pair of shoes. Would you make them?

SHOEMAKER. Well...*(She doesn't quite know how to take his question.)*

SOLDIER. This is all just suppose, now. Would you make the shoes?

SHOEMAKER *(thinking it over)*. They would fetch a handsome price, would they not?

SOLDIER. Naturally. *(He watches the SHOEMAKER craftily.)*

SHOEMAKER *(becoming more animated as she sells the imaginary shoes)*. Why, I could say to the customer, "Here is a pair of shoes that will last forever. Walk, run, climb, dance in them, they will never wear out..." *(She is struck with a new thought.)* Ah, but if he bought the shoes, he would never have to buy another. I couldn't make a living that way.

SOLDIER. But think what would happen when it became known throughout the countryside that you had made such a pair of shoes.

SHOEMAKER *(slowly realizing the implication of such a fame)*. Why—I would become famous! And naturally, I could begin to charge more for ordinary shoes! *(She considers that for a moment, very pleased, and then comes down to earth again. However, the OLD SOLDIER is satisfied with her cupidity.)* Ah, Old Soldier, you talk of impossible things. Imagine a pair of shoes that don't wear out!

KIRSTEN. My father could never afford to buy such wonderful shoes.

THORA. Nor mine.

MARTA. They would have to be magic shoes.

SHOEMAKER. Indeed they would!

(KAREN enters slowly, shyly, from DR. She is carrying a very ragged soiled doll. Her clothes are ragged and dusty. Her face, arms, and legs are smudged, and her hair uncombed. She should not be so unkempt as to be repulsive—she is a waif of the streets who has not become hardened because of neglect. She is barefoot. She stands apart from the OTHERS, and the CHILDREN do not

see her. The OLD SOLDIER does, however, and looks her over calculatingly. It is apparent from KAREN's attitude that she longs to be accepted by them.)

KIRSTEN *(whirling around).* If I were to have magic shoes, I would want shoes that would make me dance gracefully and lightly, like the leaves that rustle in the wind.

HANS *(striding about).* I would want my magic shoes to be like seven league boots, so I could stride from village to village in single steps.

NILS. I would be happy if I could have shoes that don't pinch my feet.

OLUF. Or shoes that never need to be shined.

KRISTINE. I would want shoes so full of magic that I would never grow tired.

KAREN *(pulled into the discussion in spite of her timidity).* I'd like shoes like the Princess wears.

INGE. Well, Karen dirty-face! Listen to her fine talk!

THORA. She wants the shoes of a Princess when she doesn't have any shoes at all!

KAREN. I can wish for them, can't I? Even though I know I'll never have shoes as nice as those. *(She points wistfully to the drab shoes on the cart.)*

SHOEMAKER *(sensing a sale, pushing her cart R, to KAREN).* And why not, Miss? Tell me where you live and I will sell your mother any shoes you may want—if she has ten crowns. *(As KAREN does not answer.)* Well, what's the matter?

KAREN. I have no mother to buy me shoes. All the shoes I've ever had are those I have dreamed about. Shoes of gold, and of silver, shoes with shining jewels sewn upon them, shoes fit for a Princess.

INGE *(with a mock curtsy)*. Karen, the barefoot Princess!

KIRSTEN *(in ridicule)*. Shoes fit for a Princess!

MARTA. How do you know what kind of shoes the Princess wears?

KAREN. Well—I don't.

SOLDIER. I know what kind of shoes the Princess wears.

CHILDREN *(ad lib)*. You do?

SHOEMAKER. Ah, Old Soldier, how would you know anything about the Princess?

SOLDIER. I know this about the Princess. I know that today she is going to travel the road yonder below this hill.

CHILDREN *(ad lib)*. She is? *(They rush to the wall C and look.)*

KIRSTEN. I don't see any Princess.

SOLDIER. I didn't say you would see the Princess this instant. All I said was that she will be passing by here some time today.

SHOEMAKER. How do you know that, old man?

SOLDIER *(evasively)*. There are ways of knowing these things, to those who know how to know.

MARTA. Is she really coming?

ALICE. To our village?

SOLDIER. Shoot me for a deserter if I am not telling you the truth. *(He is very sure of himself.)*

KAREN *(eagerly)*. Then I will see the kind of shoes the Princess wears?

SOLDIER. Perhaps.

SHOEMAKER. Old Soldier, you are full of fanciful tales. Don't believe him, children. He has been too close to the noise of booming cannon and cannot think straight.

SOLDIER *(peering intently into her face)*. Look me in the eyes and tell me I can't think straight. You don't know who I am, do you?

SHOEMAKER *(walking away from him with an impatient gesture)*. Bah!

KAREN *(excitedly, from her place at the gate, where she has been looking off UL, as though seeing the road to Copenhagen in the distance)*. Look, I see a great cloud of dust on the road yonder! *(The CHILDREN exclaim and rush to the wall to see. They stay at the wall, looking out, during the next scene.)*

SOLDIER. The Princess, no doubt.

SHOEMAKER *(reprovingly)*. Why do you fool the children with all this nonsense about the Princess?

SOLDIER. I am not fooling. *(He regards the SHOEMAKER quizzically and then crosses to her swiftly. He speaks urgently, but so the CHILDREN cannot overhear him.)* I will make a wager with you.

SHOEMAKER *(warily)*. What kind of a wager?

SOLDIER. Simply this. You do not believe me when I say the Princess will come here today. If she does come by, you are to make a pair of shoes to my order.

SHOEMAKER *(puzzled)*. Make a pair of shoes?

SOLDIER. You know how to make shoes, don't you? I said, if the Princess comes by you are to make a pair of shoes to my order—and I will even furnish the leather. *(He does not indicate from where he will get the leather.)*

SHOEMAKER. I understand. But what happens if the Princess does *not* come by?

SOLDIER. If she does not come by, I will give you what is in my knapsack.

SHOEMAKER. Which may be filled with straw for aught I know.

SOLDIER. You are a mistrustful soul. *(He opens his knapsack.)*

SHOEMAKER *(peering in the knapsack, and making a move as though to touch its contents.)* Beautiful! Where did you get that red...

SOLDIER *(pulling the knapsack from her reach)*. Sshhh! *(With a gesture toward the CHILDREN.)* This is between you and me only. Well, is it a wager? *(He tempts her craftily showing the contents of the knapsack, this time pulling out a corner of a piece of red leather. He allows her to feel it.)*

SHOEMAKER *(as she feels the leather)*. If the Princess does not come, this leather is mine?

SOLDIER. That is right.

SHOEMAKER. *(She feels it again, looks at the OLD SOLDIER, steps to the wall and looks down the road. Satisfied with what she does not see there, she returns to the OLD SOLDIER.)* Done. I will make the pair of shoes if the Princess comes.

SOLDIER. Done. *(He tucks the leather back in the knapsack and turns to the CHILDREN.)* Can you see her?

THORA. The road is hidden by a hill.

OLUF. We can't see a thing.

INGE. Karen must have been seeing things.

KAREN. I *did* seen a cloud of dust on the road.

SOLDIER. Of course you did. Come, let us dance for the Princess!

CHILDREN *(ad lib)*. Dance for the Princess?

SOLDIER. Of course! This is the way it will be. There will be a great blowing of trumpets. Up to the gate will come footmen and ladies in waiting. Then, with a great fanfare, the gate will open and the Princess will come in. We all bow low. The Princess acknowledges us. She sees the pipe in my hand. Would we dance for her if I will be kind enough to play? Of course! So the Princess seats herself there *(He places KAREN on the bench by the tree.)* and we dance for her. *(As he speaks, the OLD SOLDIER and the CHILDREN enact the scene in pantomime. When the CHILDREN form a circle to dance, KAREN springs up from the bench to join them, but she is shouldered away. So while the CHILDREN dance "The Seven Jumps"—see Production Notes —KAREN sits disconsolately on the wall R, alternately watching the DANCERS and the road. As the dance is almost over, she spies what she is looking for.)*

KAREN *(excitedly)*. She's here! She's here! The Princess! *(The CHILDREN rush to the wall to see.)*

SOLDIER *(to the SHOEMAKER)*. I told you.

KIRSTEN. Look, her carriage is stopping!

MARTA. She's right below us!

INGE. Let's go down to see her!

HANS. Come on!

THORA. Hurry! *(The CHILDREN exit, ad lib, via the gate, pushing KAREN rudely out of the way.)*

SOLDIER *(to the SHOEMAKER, tantalizingly)*. She not only passes by, as I said she would, but stops so you can see she *is* the Princess.

SHOEMAKER. You must be the devil himself to know what is going to happen before it happens.

SOLDIER. I will not take offense at what you say. *(To KAREN, who stands at the gate.)* Are you not going down to see her?

KAREN. No.

SOLDIER. Why not? You wanted to see the Princess... and her shoes.

KAREN. I can see her from here. Down there, I would just be pushed out of the way. It's always like that. People don't want to have anything to do with a ragamuffin like me...with no shoes.

SOLDIER. Would you like a pair of shoes, child?

KAREN. Oh, yes!

SOLDIER. What color would you like?

KAREN. What color? Are not all shoes black?

SOLDIER. There are other colors. *(He leaves her abruptly and goes to the SHOEMAKER.)* The Princess is below. You have lost your wager. You must now make me a pair of shoes.

SHOEMAKER. That is so. But you furnish the leather, remember?

SOLDIER. I do not forget. *(Tosses her his knapsack.)* Use the leather in my knapsack.

SHOEMAKER *(greedily, surprised)*. You mean I should use the red...

SOLDIER. Ssh! And I want it—at once. *(Peering at her intently.)*

SHOEMAKER *(as though hypnotized)*. At once, of course. *(She is almost off-stage when she turns.)* What size?

SOLDIER. The size will not matter. Not when you use *my* leather. *(SHOEMAKER nods and goes with her cart and the knapsack, L. SOLDIER, to KAREN.)* And now, Karen, if you so wish, you may have your shoes...of such a beautiful color that everyone will say, "See Karen's shoes. There are no others like them in all the world!"

KAREN. Do...do you...mean what you say?

SOLDIER. Of course I mean what I say!

KAREN *(appealingly)*. What do I have to *do* to get shoes like that?

SOLDIER. Listen to what I have to say, Karen, and you shall have them. Shoes in which to walk, to run, to dance...!

KAREN. To dance! *(Almost too much to believe.)*

(As KAREN and the OLD SOLDIER are lost in the thought of the meaning of the shoes, the FOOTMAN enters at the gate. He is a foppish young man, very much taken with himself and his service to the PRINCESS.)

FOOTMAN *(clapping his hands)*. Her most gracious Highness, the Princess, desires that this courtyard be emptied of all people. Remove yourselves.

SOLDIER. To whom are you talking?

FOOTMAN. To you, rabble. Come, out with you.

SOLDIER. Fop.

FOOTMAN. Dare you so to disobey the Princess? *(To KAREN.)* Child, you heard me?

KAREN *(timidly)*. I would like to see the Princess.

FOOTMAN. 'Tis a compliment the Princess would not care to return, I'm sure. *(Shooing KAREN.)* Out, out, out!...*(Turning to the OLD SOLDIER.)* Be off with you, lest the Princess be displeased.

SOLDIER. I can't see that my being here is any of her business.

FOOTMAN *(exasperated)*. The Princess gave express orders to clear away all people who may be here. She wishes to see this quaint rustic church undisturbed.

SOLDIER *(startled)*. The church? *(He glances at the church almost distastefully and rises.)* I will respect her wishes. *(He goes out R, quickly.)*

FOOTMAN *(to KAREN)*. Now you! Leave!

KAREN. But I want to see the Princess.

FOOTMAN. Of course, everyone wants to see the Princess. *(Sarcastically.)* Or do you have some special reason to see her?

KAREN. I want to see her shoes.

FOOTMAN. Her shoes! I will speak to her bootblack about it. Now out with you before I suffer the indignity of chasing you out. *(KAREN stands firm, so he makes a feint as though to chase her. KAREN runs a few steps. He continues to feint, with KAREN evasively side-stepping him, until he is forced to give full chase to get KAREN out.)* Oh! My breath!

(The FOOTMAN regains his composure, checks the courtyard, and goes to the gate, where he beckons as though to another footman down the hill. He waits. The PRINCESS and her LADY enter after a pause.)

PRINCESS. Thank you, Thomas. You may leave us now.

FOOTMAN. Your Highness will not be long? We are well behind our schedule.

PRINCESS. Just a few minutes. Go, please. *(FOOTMAN leaves by the gate.)* Do this, do that, you're not on time. Oh, to be like the girls who crowd around my coach.

LADY. But your Highness, you would not then be the Princess.

PRINCESS *(eagerly)*. Let me forget my royal duties for just these few moments. Is it not peaceful and quiet here?

LADY. It is, your Highness.

PRINCESS. We are *alone*, my Lady! There are no voices shouting my name. No one is watching me, and I don't have to behave like a Princess. I could stay here the rest of the afternoon! *(She sprawls on the bench in an un-princess-like manner.)*

LADY. And do nothing, your Highness?

PRINCESS *(enjoying the idea hugely)*. And do nothing—nothing at all. *(She looks about her, notices the tree.)* See how the leaves dance in the breeze? *(Impulsively.)* Come, my lady, dance with me.

LADY. But your Highness...

PRINCESS *(in Princess-like manner in spite of herself)*. I would dance, your Ladyship.

LADY *(curtsying)*. As you command, your Highness.

PRINCESS. Oh, no, no, no! You spoil it all. I ask that you dance, in the manner of a simple peasant girl, and you say, "As you command." Everything is at my command! *(Wistfully.)* Can't people ever do things with me because it might be fun?

LADY. I am sorry, your Highness. I cannot forget you are a Princess.

PRINCESS. No, I suppose not. *(She looks at her dress.)* Perhaps I should dirty my dress, smudge my face, and kick off my shoes...I wonder how it would feel to have the cool stones beneath my feet, and the warm dust between my toes.

LADY. The stones would be rough, I'm afraid, and the dust would cause you to have many a footbath.

PRINCESS. But with my dress in rags, and a smudged face, I wouldn't be a Princess, and when I wished to dance, others would dance with me because they wanted to! *(She pirouettes. A VOICE, off, sings "Rosalille," as though approaching and going away. See Production Notes.)* Listen! How happy and carefree she sounds.

(The PRINCESS listens, goes over to her LADY, taking her hand, and soon both are dancing. As they dance, KAREN enters and watches, noticing the PRINCESS's red shoes. When the dance is finished, she hugs the corner of the church, where she can see, but can withdraw into the shadows when she fears discovery.)

LADY *(as the singing fades away)*. Oh, your Highness, is that what you meant?

PRINCESS. Yes...and no. That was too stately. I would love to dance the kind of dance that whirls me about, faster and faster, until I was exhausted from delight. *(She whirls about and stops in front of the church door with a guilty start.)* Oh, the church!

LADY. Yes, your Highness. We came here to look at it.

PRINCESS. Oh, yes. Isn't it lovely? How quaint and simple it is. *(She admires the church from several angles, then impetuously runs up the steps.)* Let us go in.

LADY. Oh, your Highness, you cannot!

PRINCESS *(regally)*. Cannot?

LADY. I mean, your Highness has on red shoes. Have we not learned that red is the color of the devil, and is not a fit color to be taken into the house of the Lord?

PRINCESS. You see, I had almost forgotten I am a Princess. *(She looks at her shoes, lifting her skirts a bit. Then quickly, impulsively, she slips her shoes off, and places them neatly on the top step.)* There! Now I am properly dressed to go into church.

LADY. Your Highness! In your bare feet!

PRINCESS *(defensively)*. Not quite bare. I have stockings on. I have never heard that one could not go into a church without shoes.

LADY. N-n-n-o.

PRINCESS. Besides, no one is here to see us. Come. *(Holds out her hand invitingly.)* If you do not come, I'll go myself.

LADY *(giving in)*. I will go with you.

(The PRINCESS and her LADY enter the church, leaving the shoes on the church step, in full view. KAREN comes out of her hiding place and circles around, staring at the shoes all the time, until she is on the U end of the steps.)

KAREN. The Princess' shoes! The Princess wears red shoes! *(She goes slowly up the steps and sits next to the shoes. She does not touch them.)* Oh, if I had shoes, I would want them to be red.

(The OLD SOLDIER appears behind the wall, where he watches KAREN.)

KAREN *(propping up her doll and speaking to it)*. I would be a real Princess, if I had red shoes. *(She sits erectly, with a regal pose.)* I would sit like this, and people would have to bow before me, while my red shoes would shine.

SOLDIER. Do you think you would be happy, Karen?

KAREN *(startled)*. Oh!

SOLDIER. Do you think you would be happy, just sitting like a Princess? Wouldn't you want to dance in your red shoes?

KAREN. Dance?

SOLDIER. Yes. If you had red shoes, you could dance.

KAREN. I could be a Princess, and dance, too.

SOLDIER. You could. Karen, listen! There are shoes, right there. Red shoes. Why don't you take them?

KAREN. Oh!

SOLDIER. Take the shoes and run.

KAREN. I couldn't.

SOLDIER. Don't be a little fool. There they are, for the taking. Shoes for Karen, for a Karen who would be a Princess, shoes for dancing...

(The OLD SOLDIER takes his pipe and plays "The Shoemaker's Dance" music. As he plays, he looks carelessly away, glancing from time to time to see what KAREN is going to do. Slowly, she goes to the top step, bends down, and picks up the shoes, leaving her doll on the steps. As KAREN starts down the steps, wonderingly, holding the shoes to her body, the FOOTMAN enters.)

FOOTMAN. Your Highness, it is time to leave. *(He notices KAREN in a frozen attitude.)* Where is the Princess? *(Notices the shoes in KAREN's hands.)* The Princess' red shoes! What are you doing with the Princess' shoes?! *(He seizes KAREN by the arm.)*

KAREN. I just...I wasn't...

FOOTMAN *(loudly)*. Thief! Thief! *(To KAREN, working his way to the gate as she resists.)* You little thief. You'll get yours! Thief! Help, here, I have a thief!

(In the struggle, KAREN stumbles and falls to the ground, Right of Center, still held by the FOOTMAN. PRINCESS and the LADY come out of the church in response to the turmoil. The OLD SOLDIER continues to watch the scene from behind the wall.)

PRINCESS. What is it? *(As she sees her FOOTMAN.)* Thomas! What are you shouting about?

FOOTMAN. This little ragamuffin was stealing your shoes.

PRINCESS. My shoes? Oh...*(She starts toward KAREN, noticing her for the first time.)* A dirty dress, a smudged face, and no shoes...*(The PRINCESS sounds so kindly that KAREN raises her eyes to look at her.)* She won't run away, Thomas. Let her go...*(She stoops to talk to KAREN.)* What is your name?

KAREN. Karen.

PRINCESS. You like my shoes, Karen?

KAREN. I...I didn't know what I was doing. They are beautiful shoes.

PRINCESS. Why did you want my shoes?

KAREN. I have never had a pair of shoes in all my life.

PRINCESS *(big-eyed)*. Hasn't your mother, or your father, ever bought you a pair of shoes?

KAREN. I don't remember ever having a father. And my mother...I have no mother anymore, either. Not since last Christmas.

PRINCESS. Where do you live? Who takes care of you?

KAREN. I just go from village to village and take care of myself.

LADY. An orphan, your Highness.

PRINCESS. Oh...*(Helplessly, she stands up and turns inquiringly to the LADY.)*

KAREN. I am sorry I tried to take your shoes, Princess. *(She extends the shoes to the PRINCESS. FOOTMAN grabs the shoes. KAREN rises and begins to go, R.)*

FOOTMAN. Your shoes, your Highness. We are very late.

PRINCESS. Karen, don't go.

KAREN. But I tried to steal your shoes!

PRINCESS *(going to KAREN)*. Once upon a time, Karen, when I was a little girl, I wanted to wear a diamond necklace. So one day, I went to my mother's jewel box and took the biggest, shiniest diamond necklace I could find. I thought that if I wanted something badly enough, I could help myself. Well, I was caught—and I learned then that taking things is not the way to get things we might want. *(The PRINCESS and KAREN smile at each other in understanding.)*

FOOTMAN. What are we to do with her, your Highness?

PRINCESS. I don't know.

LADY *(who has been considering the situation)*. Your Highness, I remember hearing it said in Copenhagen that in this village there lives a grandmother who gives a home to children who need a home. Perhaps...

PRINCESS *(eagerly)*. Are you sure she lives in this village?

LADY. Yes, I am quite sure. I think her name is Grandmother Nissen.

PRINCESS. Thomas, seek out this woman. Tell her the Princess asks her to come to the church courtyard to find Karen and to give her a home. *(She slips her ring from her finger.)* Here is my ring as your authority.

FOOTMAN *(not wanting to go)*. You want me to go now, your Highness?

PRINCESS. At once. When you have completed this errand, join us again. *(Turns to KAREN.)* Karen, you are to wait here for Grandmother Nissen.

KAREN. Will she get me shoes—red shoes?

PRINCESS *(kindly)*. I am sure she will get you shoes. *(To the lingering FOOTMAN.)* Go now, Thomas.

FOOTMAN *(turning to go, and discovering the shoes still in his hands, shoves them toward the LADY, who takes them and gives them to the PRINCESS)*. This is most irregular. *(He goes via the gate.)*

PRINCESS *(putting on her shoes)*. Remember, Karen, you are to wait here for her. She will come. Good-bye.

KAREN. Good-bye, and thank you.

PRINCESS. Oh, my Lady, how glad I am that we stopped here! *(KAREN and the PRINCESS wave to each other as the PRINCESS goes, followed by the LADY. KAREN runs and watches them go down the hill.)*

SOLDIER *(after a pause, and from behind the wall)*. You little fool! Why didn't' you run when you had the shoes in your hands?!

KAREN *(going away from him)*. Don't you talk to me any more. I won't listen to you!

SOLDIER *(vehemently)*. Yes you will listen, Karen! *(He comes into the courtyard.)*

KAREN. I will not! Grandmother Nissen is coming to take care of me. She'll get me shoes!

SOLDIER. Bah! She'll get you shoes, all right. Big black clodhoppers, or wooden shoes. Wouldn't you rather have red shoes, Karen? Like the Princess? Ah, you listen to me, Karen, and you shall have shoes, red shoes...

KAREN. I won't listen to you! I won't steal shoes!

SOLDIER *(blandly)*. Who said anything about stealing? There are other ways of getting red shoes, believe me.

KAREN *(interested)*. What way?

SOLDIER. You will know, when the time comes. Just be listening to what I may have to say.

KAREN. But why don't you tell me now?

SOLDIER *(hearing the VOICES of the CHILDREN below).* There is not time for you to hear now. But remember this—even if you do not see me, you will hear me, inside. *(He points significantly to his heart and to his head.)* Remember!

KAREN. I'll be listening! *(The OLD SOLDIER goes off quickly. KAREN looks off after him, then runs to her doll, hugs it to her, and talks to it.)* Did you hear that? The old soldier says I'm going to get shoes—red shoes, like the Princess', and I won't have to steal them, either! Oh, you poor little thing, maybe you'll get some shoes, too! *(She hears the CHILDREN approaching.)* Red shoes—red shoes!

(KAREN quickly goes DL and hides in the shadow of the church, where she looks on. The CHILDREN enter, talking.)

MARTA. Wasn't she the prettiest Princess you ever saw?

NILS. Never saw a Princess before.

INGE. Her dress! All silk!

HANS. I wish I could drive her horses. How they pranced!

OLUF. Such a carriage. It had golden handles on the door.

THORA. Did you see her shoes?

KRISTINE. Red! Red shoes!

ALICE. Of the softest leather. Weren't they dainty?

KIRSTEN. I never, never thought I'd ever be that close to a Princess.

THORA. We probably never will again.

INGE. Isn't it funny how that old soldier knew she was coming here today?

NILS. I wonder how he knew.

ALICE. Who is he, anyway?

HANS. He says he is an old soldier.

OLUF. My father says you'll find old soldiers like that wandering around from village to village. They don't know what to do with themselves.

KIRSTEN. I wish he'd come back. I liked his music.

KRISTINE. It just makes you want to dance, the way he plays.

(KAREN comes out from her hiding place.)

INGE *(noticing KAREN)*. Well, here is the barefoot Princess again. It was a good thing you had sense enough to stay away when the Princess was here.

THORA. She wouldn't have had anything to do with a ragamuffin like you.

KAREN *(friendly)*. She did, though.

ALICE. What do you mean?

KAREN *(matter-of-fact)*. I saw the Princess.

KIRSTEN. Sent you away, I'll bet.

KAREN *(remembering with pleasure)*. No, she did not. She talked to me. And what's more, she even touched me. M'mmmmmm, she smelled good!

NILS *(derisively)*. Listen to her stories!

KAREN *(beginning to defend herself)*. It's true! And I held her shoes, right in my hands, and I'm going to get shoes, just like them, from Grandmother Nissen. The Princess is sending Grandmother Nissen to get me...

OLUF *(unbelievingly)*. Grandmother Nissen!

MARTA *(in some awe)*. She gives candy bonbons to children!

THORA. Who said she is coming for you?

KAREN *(matter-of-fact again)*. The Princess.

HANS. Where is she, then?

KRISTINE. Yes, where is she?

KAREN *(in faith)*. She will come, the Princess said.

INGE. The way she can make up stories.

THORA. You don't even know Grandmother Nissen.

KAREN *(stoutly)*. The Princess said she will come.

KIRSTEN. The Princess wouldn't have anything to do with the likes of you.

INGE. Such a story. First she sees the Princess. Then she talks to her. Next she holds the Princess' shoes. Then she says Grandmother Nissen is coming to get her.

ALICE. How could you hold the Princess' shoes when she was wearing them?

CHILDREN *(ad lib)*. That's right! How could you hold them? Were you holding her feet? *(Etc.)*

KAREN *(heatedly, stung to anger)*. Well, she wasn't wearing them, if you want to know. The Princess' shoes were there. *(She points to the top of the church steps.)* She took them off when she went inside, because her Lady said red was the color of the devil and she shouldn't wear red shoes to church. While she was in the church, I went up the steps, and...*(She has re-enacted the scene and is now standing where she had picked up the shoes.)*...and I picked them up...to...to look at them. *(She remembers guiltily why she had picked them up, so she finishes her story defensively.)*

OLUF. She was stealing the Princess' shoes.

HANS. Sure she was!

KIRSTEN. Thief!

THORA. And she's made up that story about Grandmother Nissen.

INGE. More likely the Princess has sent for the constable to have her arrested.

OLUF. Let's guard the gate and the street so she can't get away! *(HANS, NILS, and OLUF each choose between the gate and the two street entrances, and run there with some of the GIRLS in an attitude of guarding.)*

INGE *(chanting)*. Karen, Karen dirty face, Karen, Karen dirty face! *(The CHILDREN take up the chant, and repeat it over and over. KAREN makes a break to run out the gate, but is met with the CHILDREN there. She runs DR, and is similarly rebuffed; then DL, and cannot get out. This is not a physical encounter—she knows she could not break through the cordon guarding each exit. Finally, she stands C, trapped, her eyes searching for a way out. She spies the church door, and she bounds up the steps in triumph.)*

KAREN *(on the top step, outshouting the CHILDREN)*. You can't trap me! When Grandmother Nissen comes, tell her I'm in the church! *(She runs into the church. The CHILDREN cease their chant and gasp in shock and astonishment.)*

KRISTINE. She went in the church!

INGE. Barefoot—in the church!

THORA. How dare she go in without being dressed up!

HANS. Let's go in and drag her out! *(He strides to the steps.)*

MARTA *(facing him)*. We can't do that.

HANS. Yes, we can. She shouldn't be in there the way she is. *(Some of the CHILDREN are up the steps, ready to go. Some are unsure of themselves. Others are sure they don't want to go.)*

MARTA. We can't drag anyone out of a church. I was reading in my history book that a church is a...a sanctuary.

OLUF. What's that?

KIRSTEN. Marta's right. A sanctuary is a place where in the olden days people who had done wrong could hide, even from the constable, and couldn't be arrested.

HANS. I don't believe it.

ALICE. It's so. I remember reading about it.

HANS. Well, this isn't the olden days. I'm going in and drag her out, see?

(HANS swaggers to the door and opens it just as GRANDMOTHER NISSEN, the NURSE, and the FOOTMAN enter from the gate. His ardor cools at once. The CHILDREN all look "caught.")

GRANDMOTHER *(unseeing, but trying to see)*. Is this the place?

FOOTMAN. This is it.

GRANDMOTHER. Thank goodness. I'm all out of breath. Do you see her?

NURSE. There are some children here, but I don't see a ragged one. *(She has seated GRANDMOTHER at the bench at the tree.)*

GRANDMOTHER. Ask them.

NURSE. Have you seen a girl named Karen? *(The CHILDREN disperse slowly from the church door. They feel very guilty—and also somewhat dumbfounded to see that KAREN has told the truth. NURSE, in good humor.)* Well, can't you speak? Grandmother Nissen is looking for a girl named Karen.

INGE. She...she's in there. *(She indicates the church.)*

NURSE *(surprised)*. In the church?

GRANDMOTHER *(pleased)*. I don't often find my little street urchins in a church. That is a good omen, Nurse. Go fetch her.

NURSE *(going to the church door and calling softly)*. Karen!...Karen!...Grandmother Nissen is here for you. *(She looks into the church, and we see her looking down as though seeing KAREN hiding.)* What are you doing under the pews, child? There isn't anything to be afraid of. Come and meet Grandmother Nissen.

(The NURSE holds out her hand. There is a pause, and slowly KAREN comes out of the door. She looks half fearfully at the NURSE.)

NURSE. Here she is.

FOOTMAN *(with distaste)*. That's the one. *(KAREN looks at GRANDMOTHER, and cannot help giving a look of triumph at the CHILDREN.)*

GRANDMOTHER. Come here, child. *(As KAREN hesitates.)* Karen, where are you?

NURSE *(gently)*. Go to her, Karen. She is almost blind and cannot see very well. *(KAREN goes slowly to the GRANDMOTHER and stands before her.)*

KAREN. Here I am...Grandmother.

GRANDMOTHER. Let me look at you. *(She squints at KAREN.)* What color are your eyes?

KAREN. They are blue—Grandmother. *(Or whatever color her eyes may be.)*

GRANDMOTHER. Is she very dirty, Nurse?

NURSE *(judiciously)*. Well, we have had dirtier ones.

GRANDMOTHER *(feeling of KAREN)*. Your clothes are in rags! Well, you will get clean clothes—petticoats, dresses, stockings...

KAREN *(eagerly)*. And shoes?

GRANDMOTHER. Of course. Do you mean to tell me you do not have shoes?

KAREN *(simply)*. No, Grandmother. I have no shoes. *(Off R, we hear the SHOEMAKER chanting her wares.)*

SHOEMAKER *(off, approaching)*. Get your shoes, get your shoes. Shoes for feet both big and small. Get your shoes, get your shoes. Shoes that hardly wear at all.

(The SHOEMAKER enters with her cart. On top of her black drab shoes is the pair of red shoes, where no one can miss seeing them.)

SHOEMAKER *(expansively)*. Good day, madame and mistress. Are you in need of shoes?

GRANDMOTHER *(delighted)*. We talk about shoes, and the shoe peddler appears! One moment, good woman. *(To KAREN.)* Karen, do you wish to stay in my home?

KAREN *(her eyes fastened on the red shoes)*. If I may have shoes, oh, yes.

GRANDMOTHER. All right, then. We will buy your shoes right now...Oh, dear, I left my purse in the coach. *(She squints to see the NURSE.)* Nurse...who is that person with you? *(As she notices the figure of the FOOTMAN.)*

FOOTMAN *(with forced patience)*. Footman to her Highness, the Princess.

GRANDMOTHER. What are you waiting around for? Tell the Princess I have found Karen and am taking her in. Here is her ring. I give you leave to go.

FOOTMAN *(released from his menial task at last)*. I am grateful. *(He goes.)*

GRANDMOTHER. Nurse, run down and get my purse. It must be in the carriage. *(The NURSE leaves via the gate.)* Now, Shoemaker, do you have sturdy black leather shoes for this child?

SHOEMAKER. That I have.

GRANDMOTHER. Shoes that will give a good twelve-month of wear?

SHOEMAKER. My shoes will wear as long as any.

GRANDMOTHER. Karen, pick yourself out a pair of shoes.

KAREN. Any pair?

GRANDMOTHER. Any pair. Make a good choice, now.

KAREN *(hesitating only for the moment it takes her to realize that a dream is coming true)*. Those. *(She points to the red shoes. The CHILDREN look at one another. The SHOEMAKER glances around to find the OLD SOLDIER.)*

SHOEMAKER. Those shoes are...

KAREN. She said any pair, and that's the pair I want.

SHOEMAKER. Yes, but those shoes are...

GRANDMOTHER. Give Karen the shoes she has picked out, Shoemaker.

SHOEMAKER. Yes, madame. But I ought to tell you, madame...

KAREN *(with just a shade of Princess-like imperiality)*. You said any pair, Grandmother, and those are the ones I want.

GRANDMOTHER *(indulgently)*. Of course. And those are the ones you shall have. Are they good-looking black shoes?

KAREN *(after a moment's hesitation)*. They are beautiful...black shoes, shiny and black. *(With meaning, toward the SHOEMAKER. The CHILDREN whisper, "Oooh, she lied!" among themselves, and follow the scene with growing jealousy, for they see KAREN getting what she wants.)*

GRANDMOTHER. Give me the shoes, Shoemaker.

SHOEMAKER *(shrugging off her responsibility)*. Well...if Karen says they are black shoes, here are the black shoes. *(She hands the red shoes to GRANDMOTHER.)*

GRANDMOTHER *(exclaiming in surprise and pleasure as she feels the shoes)*. I have not felt such quality leather since I was a young woman. *(She feels the shoes and reminisces.)* It was in Copenhagen, just before my wedding. I saw a pair of shoes in a shop window. My mother said we wouldn't buy shoes there, but the more she said "no," the more I wanted those shoes. Finally, my mother gave in. They felt like these, leather as soft as silk. I wore them to the dance after my wedding. *(She pauses, and her pleasant memories fade.)* After the dance, on the way home, the horses became frightened and ran away. The carriage was overturned...my husband was killed, and I have been nearly blind ever since. I couldn't bring myself to wear those shoes again, and I threw them away. *(She pauses again, lost in her tragic memory, when she is struck with a fearful thought.)* These shoes—they are not the same shoes, Shoemaker? *(There is a note of panic in her voice.)*

SHOEMAKER *(pointedly)*. They are new shoes, madame. I just finished making them.

GRANDMOTHER. Of course. And besides, these shoes are black, and my shoes were...*(She breaks her line of thought.)* It was foolish of me to think that anything will happen to Karen because she wants shoes so badly. *(Briskly.)* How much are they?

SHOEMAKER *(calculatingly)*. One hundred crowns.

GRANDMOTHER. Why, shoes like these would cost another fifty crowns in Copenhagen! *(She holds them out and peers at them, trying to see.)* I can see them shine! *(KAREN becomes apprehensive.)*

(NURSE enters.)

NURSE. Here is your purse, Grandmother.

GRANDMOTHER. Pay the shoemaker, please. One hundred crowns.

NURSE. One hundred...!

GRANDMOTHER. Yes, our Karen is getting a pair of shoes such as we have never seen in this countryside. She picked them out herself. *(Shows the shoes.)* Are they not beautiful?

NURSE *(looking at the shoes, then to the pleased face of the GRANDMOTHER, to KAREN, and the SHOEMAKER, who shrugs her shoulders eloquently)*. Yes... they are beautiful. Here is the hundred crowns. *(She counts out the money.)*

GRANDMOTHER. Well, then, Karen, here are your shoes. *(She gives KAREN the shoes.)* Mind you keep them clean and well shined.

KAREN *(radiant)*. Oh, I will, Grandmother. And thank you! *(As she takes the shoes, she puts her doll on the bench at the tree.)*

NURSE. She is all paid, Grandmother.

GRANDMOTHER. Then let us go.

NURSE. Come, Karen. *(The NURSE, GRANDMOTHER, and KAREN exit via the gate. The CHILDREN seem too stunned to speak. SOME of them go to the gate to see KAREN go. The SHOEMAKER is greedily recounting her money at the extreme Right.)*

INGE *(bursting out)*. Did you hear how she lied?

THORA. Called the red shoes black!

INGE. She'll get it when Grandmother Nissen finds out!

KIRSTEN. How will she find out. She can't see.

OLUF. We ought to tell her.

HANS. All right! Let's go. *(There is a movement among the CHILDREN toward the gate, when we hear KAREN off, as though halfway up the hill.)*

KAREN *(off)*. I'll be right down. I forgot my doll!

NURSE *(faintly, off)*. All right. Hurry along.

HANS. She's coming back for her doll! Ssshhh!

(HANS puts his finger over his mouth and stands stiffly against the wall to the Right of the gate pillar. He motions the other CHILDREN to stand back. OLUF snatches up the doll as KAREN enters, carrying her red shoes. She stops as she sees the hostile CHILDREN. She does not see HANS.)

KAREN *(to OLUF)*. I'd like my doll, please. *(She looks from CHILD to CHILD, as OLUF pretends not to hear and plays with the doll mockingly.)*

INGE *(finally breaking the silence)*. Liar!

ALICE. Oh, what a liar!

KAREN *(fearfully)*. You won't tell on me...please? I never had a pair of shoes before...and they are so pretty...*(As she holds them out, HANS darts out and grabs the shoes.)*

HANS *(chanting)*. Liar, liar, Karen! Liar, liar, Karen! *(The OTHER CHILDREN pick up the chant as they toss the shoes back and forth. KAREN wildly tries to rescue them. OLUF drops the doll to the ground and joins in the melee.)*

KAREN. My shoes! My shoes! Give me my shoes!

HANS. Come on, let's take them down to Grandmother Nissen.

(As the CHILDREN start for the gate, the OLD SOLDIER appears there. HANS is stopped short as he was in the beginning of the act.)

SOLDIER *(smoothly)*. Karen's shoes, please. *(The CHILDREN who have the shoes give them up to him sheepishly. He takes the shoes, looks them over critically. He is pleased with what he sees and nods approval at the SHOEMAKER. He wipes the shoes on his sleeve, and with a grand flourish, he hands them to KAREN.)*

KAREN *(relieved and overwhelmed with gratitude)*. Thank you! Oh, thank you! *(She takes her shoes and runs out the gate. The OLD SOLDIER watches KAREN go down the steps. He turns, and sees the doll on the ground. He picks it up, dusts it carefully, and with a knowing, crafty smile, he dances the doll, while off-stage the music of "The Shoemaker's Dance" is heard. The CHILDREN and the SHOEMAKER look upon him, puzzled by his actions.*

CURTAIN

END OF ACT ONE

ACT TWO

SETTING: *The same scene, early Sunday morning, before church services.*

AT RISE: *The curtain opens on an empty stage. Presently FRU NIELSEN enters with HANS, OLUF, KRISTINE, and INGE. The CHILDREN are dressed in their "Sunday" clothes, and seem to be more decorous in their behavior.*

FRU NIELSEN. Here we are. A little early, it seems.

INGE. I told you, Mother, that we would be too early.

FRU NIELSEN. It will not do you any harm to sit quietly for awhile and enjoy God's beautiful Sunday morning.

INGE. But we enjoy every morning, Mother.

FRU NIELSEN. Romping and dancing. I know. But this is Sunday morning, which is God's own day, and instead of romping and dancing, this is a time to be quiet and to think of your many blessings. Now sit down. A few minutes of quiet won't hurt you. *(The CHILDREN sit reluctantly on the bench C, which, while large enough, somehow does not have enough room this morning. There is considerable jostling, which changes to beatific attitudes whenever FRU NIELSEN raises her eyes from her prayer book. She is seated DR, under the tree.)* Inge, do you know your catechism lesson for today? You could be studying it, you know.

INGE. I knew it perfectly last night.

FRU NIELSEN. I hope you haven't forgotten since.

HANS. I know mine backwards and forwards.

FRU NIELSEN *(sharply)*. I'm sure knowing it forwards is good enough. It is only the devil who can recite scripture backwards.

(FRU SORENSEN enters from the gate.)

FRU SORENSEN. Come, come, don't be so slow. I've seen you run up these steps many a time. *(Sees FRU NIELSEN.)* Good morning, Fru Nielsen. I see I am not the first.

(NILS, THORA, and MARTA enter and join the OTHER CHILDREN, the GIRLS making a little group DL, the BOYS remaining on the bench. They visit in cautious whispers.)

FRU NIELSEN. The cock crowed especially early this morning.

FRU SORENSEN. It is a bad sign. *(As she sits heavily on bench, R.)* Oof-a-my! I swear those steps are getting steeper every Sunday I climb them!

FRU NIELSEN. You, too? *(Turning her attention to the CHILDREN for a moment.)* Children, be not so noisy! The steps don't take the starch out of the young ones.

FRU SORENSEN. They have energy to spare. What is new in your life?

FRU NIELSEN. The same old scratching to keep body and soul together. And with you?

FRU SORENSEN. The same, from one Sunday to the next. *(Having disposed of their philosophical comments, the two WOMEN read from their prayer books in silence. The CHILDREN, emboldened by their greater numbers and the absorption of their elders, begin a cautious conversation.)*

INGE. But of course she will come.

MARTA. How do you know?

INGE. I don't *know*, of course, but I know she'll come.

THORA. What makes you think so?

INGE. Grandmother Nissen always brings her children to church.

HANS. What are you talking about?

INGE. Karen.

HANS. Oh, she's lucky. Grandmother Nissen gives her children bonbons.

OLUF. That's lucky, all right.

INGE. I'm dying to see her.

KRISTINE. So am I.

THORA. I just can't imagine Karen clean and dressed up.

(RODHOLM enters, followed by KIRSTEN and ALICE.)

RODHOLM. Mind your manners, now; this is Sunday. Good morning, Fru Nielsen, Fru Sorensen.

VILLAGERS *(ad lib)*. Good morning.

FRU SORENSEN. How is your wife?

RODHOLM. Poorly, poorly.

FRU NIELSEN *(commiseratingly)*. She will be missed. *(FRU SORENSEN nudges her COMPANION, while RODHOLM makes his curt reply and leaves the WOMEN to stand at the gate.)*

RODHOLM. She's not gone yet.

(SHOEMAKER enters L. She is dressed in her Sunday best and, of course, is without her cart.)

SHOEMAKER. Good morning! I thought I would be late!

FRU NIELSEN *(looking her over)*. It is still early.

SHOEMAKER. I don't know which is worse, climbing those steps or taking the long way around through the village.

FRU SORENSEN *(with some malice)*. I should think you would not be too winded coming the long way.

SHOEMAKER. And why not?

FRU SORENSEN *(pointedly)*. You are not pushing your cart, you know.

SHOEMAKER *(good-naturedly)*. Oh, but when I am pushing my cart I have something to lean on. People stop me to buy shoes, and so I rest between times. But on Sunday, I just walk, and I notice the long stretch. *(She is seated on the extreme Right end of the bench under the tree.)*

FRU SORENSEN *(nonplused)*. H'm. *(After a significant exchange of looks with FRU NIELSEN.)* How is the shoe business these days?

(The OLD SOLDIER enters R, unseen by the OTHERS.)

SHOEMAKER *(carelessly)*. The same as ever.

FRU NIELSEN *(trying another tack)*. My Inge tells me you sold a pair of red shoes this week.

SHOEMAKER. Oh, that! Yes, I did.

FRU SORENSEN. And who in this village is getting so high and mighty that black shoes are not good enough?

FRU NIELSEN. Where did you get the red leather?

SHOEMAKER. Well, it was a strange happenstance. I got the leather from an old soldier. *(She discovers him standing at the Left.)* There he is now. *(The WOMEN devour him with curious looks, and the OLD SOLDIER realizes he has been seen.)*

SOLDIER *(with a courtly acknowledgment)*. A pleasant morning on which to meet. *(The CHILDREN crowd around him, talking ad lib.)*

FRU NIELSEN. Children! Raise not your voices except in praise and prayer on this day!

SOLDIER *(gently disengaging himself from the CHILDREN)*. Yes, children. *(Pointedly.)* 'Tis a day when the tongue of man should not gossip. *(He makes his way to RODHOLM at the gate, where they exchange greetings. The WOMEN take refuge from further talk in their prayer books, but covertly inspect the OLD SOLDIER.)*

FRU NIELSEN *(unable to contain her curiosity)*. Who is he? Where did he come from?

SHOEMAKER *(with a shrug)*. I don't know. He is a strange man. Not from this countryside. *(The OLD SOLDIER begins to play his pipe.)*

FRU NIELSEN *(rising in consternation)*. My good sir! What are you doing?

SOLDIER. Playing, what else?

FRU SORENSEN. 'Tis a Sunday morning!

SOLDIER. I thought the children might like to dance. Come, children! *(The CHILDREN begin forming their circle.)*

FRU SORENSEN. Stop it at once! 'Tis sinful to dance on the Lord's day!

SOLDIER. Not where I come from.

FRU NIELSEN. Then go back where you came from. In this village we keep this day holy. The devil finds enough mischief for our children without your asking them to dance on Sunday.

SOLDIER. I bow to your custom. Children, there will be no dancing for you today.

(The CHILDREN murmur their disappointment and break their half-formed circle. The SOLDIER sits serenely by himself, C. The VILLAGERS make an indignant group DR, looking from their prayer books to the SOLDIER. The NURSE and GRANDMOTHER enter.)

NURSE *(at the gate)*. Here we are, Grandmother.

GRANDMOTHER. Yes. I counted the steps. Karen?

(KAREN enters.)

KAREN. Yes, Grandmother? *(She is dressed in clean clothes, with her hair combed and beribboned, as pretty as a Princess. She wears her red shoes proudly and vainly, and she lords it over the CHILDREN by not seeing them except for triumphant glances. See Production Notes on costumes.)*

GRANDMOTHER. Go with Nurse. She will take you in to arrange for your first catechism. *(The NURSE seats her on Center bench.)*

KAREN. Yes, Grandmother. *(KAREN goes with the NURSE. All eyes are on the red shoes. On the top step, the NURSE hesitates for a moment, giving the shoes a troubled glance, but decides not to say anything in front of ALL the people. She walks with the proud KAREN into the church. The two WOMEN immediately bend their heads together for comment on the red shoes. The SHOEMAKER deigns not to have noticed. The CHILDREN come together in a group and break the silence. The SOLDIER continues to sit serenely. The GRANDMOTHER, of course, is unaware of either the color of the shoes or of the sensation the shoes have caused.)*

INGE. Did you see that?!

THORA. Red shoes—right in church!

ALICE *(indicating GRANDMOTHER)*. Ssshhh! She'll hear you!

INGE. She ought to know about it.

HANS. I don't want to be the one to tell her.

THORA *(to OLUF)*. You tell her.

OLUF. Not I.

KIRSTEN. Not I.

KRISTINE. Nor I.

INGE. Walks into church with red shoes!

FRU NIELSEN *(rising and going toward the CHILDREN)*. Children! Be quiet! What's all the commotion about?!

MARTA. Nothing.

FRU NIELSEN. Then say nothing if there is nothing to talk about. Keep the Sunday quiet.

GRANDMOTHER. Ah, children will rattle and gabble about nothing. 'Tis their way.

FRU NIELSEN *(tartly)*. I'll thank you to allow me to raise my children in my own way.

GRANDMOTHER *(taken aback)*. Goodness, I meant no harm. I am sure you are raising your children to walk in the ways of the Lord, just as I try to do with the poor homeless ones who come to me.

FRU NIELSEN *(with emphasis)*. The ways of the Lord, in my way of thinking, do not permit of rattling and gabbing about nothing on the Lord's day—any more than it is in His way to permit a child to wear red shoes to church.

GRANDMOTHER *(puzzled)*. Red shoes to church?

FRU NIELSEN. Yes, red shoes to church.

GRANDMOTHER. What is this talk about red shoes all of a sudden?

RODHOLM *(to FRU NIELSEN in a low voice)*. She has not seen them. Her eyes, you know.

FRU NIELSEN *(spitefully)*. She's not that blind. *(She rejoins FRU SORENSEN.)*

GRANDMOTHER. Tell me, good woman, is there something here that I know nothing of? *(She looks about her, trying to see.)* You will not answer me? *(She turns in the direction of the CHILDREN.)* Children speak the truth, for they are angels at heart. What is there here that I know nothing about?

INGE *(bursting out after a pause)*. It's Karen.

GRANDMOTHER. Karen?

INGE. She...she wore red shoes to church.

GRANDMOTHER. Red shoes? To church? Where would she get red shoes? I have bought her but one pair, and they were black.

FRU NIELSEN. Well, the shoes she is wearing this morning are not black. They are as red as the tail of the devil himself.

GRANDMOTHER *(unbelieving)*. Red...shoes? *(She peers around helplessly.)*

FRU NIELSEN. If you don't believe it, ask the one who sold them to you.

GRANDMOTHER. She is here, the shoemaker?...Shoemaker?

SHOEMAKER. I am here, madame, but you can't blame me...

GRANDMOTHER. You said the shoes were black.

SHOEMAKER. Oh, no, madame. I said I had black shoes. Karen picked out the red ones herself.

KRISTINE. She lied to you.

ALICE. She said they were black shoes.

INGE. She said she was going to get red shoes, like the Princess', and that's just what she did.

GRANDMOTHER. This is so?

KIRSTEN. We saw her.

THORA. She called the red shoes black and you believed her.

GRANDMOTHER. That I did, that I did. Oh, my poor Karen!

FRU NIELSEN. Poor Karen! She should be punished!

GRANDMOTHER *(gently)*. Oh, yes, she will be punished. I will have to take her red shoes away from her.

HANS. Aren't you going to give her a whipping?

GRANDMOTHER. Would a whip cut more sharply into her conscience than the denial of her prized shoes? And I beg of you—all of you—to say not a word of this to her when she comes out.

FRU NIELSEN. You're asking a lot.

GRANDMOTHER. I'm asking that you let me raise Karen in my own way, and I believe that loving kindness is the way of our Lord. *(She takes a step toward the church.)* Will someone help me, please? *(As no one goes to help her, there is a pause. Finally, RODHOLM takes her arm and guides her toward the steps. They stop as KAREN and the NURSE come out from the church.)* Why are we stopping?

RODHOLM. Karen is on the steps.

GRANDMOTHER. Oh...Thank you...Karen?

KAREN. Yes, Grandmother?

GRANDMOTHER. Did you have your catechism lesson already?

KAREN. Yes, I did, Grandmother.

GRANDMOTHER. Good. Come with me, then. We are going home.

NURSE. You're not going to church?

GRANDMOTHER. No, Nurse. Not this morning. *(As KAREN, GRANDMOTHER and the NURSE make their way toward the gate, all eyes are again on the red shoes.)*

INGE *(blurting out, unable to hold in her vengeful feelings)*. Karen is going to get it because of her shoes.

GRANDMOTHER *(pausing, and realizing she must take care of the matter at once, asks gently)*. Karen, why did you not tell me your shoes are red...*(As KAREN does not reply.)* They are red, are they not?

KAREN *(looking around her and seeing she is caught)*. They are red.

GRANDMOTHER *(gently reproving)*. You should not have worn them to church, Karen. Red shoes are for dancing.

FRU NIELSEN *(vindictively)*. They are the color of the devil.

FRU SORENSEN. They do not belong in a church.

FRU NIELSEN *(to GRANDMOTHER)*. You should make her take them off at once!

KAREN *(with spirit)*. I will not take them off!

GRANDMOTHER *(surprised at the outburst)*. Why, Karen, my child...

KAREN *(backing away, feeling trapped)*. I won't take them off, I won't, I won't. All my life I have had no shoes, and I won't take them off—never!

SOLDIER *(who has been watching the scene, rises slowly)*. It seems to me you are all talking with the tongues of the righteous, without knowing what is right. What does it matter if she wears red shoes to church?

FRU NIELSEN *(aghast)*. I never heard of such a thing!

FRU SORENSEN. Red shoes are never worn to church!

SOLDIER. Good ladies, hear me out, I beg of you.

FRU NIELSEN. You don't belong around here.

SOLDIER. Hear me out, nevertheless. I say it is nothing if Karen wears red shoes to church. The red shoes are shoes, for which I provided the leather. What is on her feet is of no great moment. What does count is what is in her heart, her mind, her soul. Is that not the way of your Lord?

GRANDMOTHER. There is truth in what he says.

FRU NIELSEN *(shocked)*. Blasphemy!

FRU SORENSEN. Such wickedness!

SOLDIER. I will prove my point. And I will make a bargain with you. If I am right, that it makes no difference that Karen wore red shoes to church, you are to allow her to wear them wherever and whenever she wishes, and I will leave your village as quietly as I came. But if the wearing of her red shoes can be proved to be wicked...

KAREN. I will not give them up! Never!

SOLDIER *(knowingly)*. You will not have to give up your shoes, Karen. Just tell me what was in your catechism lesson today? *(KAREN is silent and stricken.)* You were in the church, you know. Remember? Your lesson was, "In the beginning, there was..." *(He pauses.)*

KAREN *(suddenly remembering, after a pause)*. Nothing! There was nothing!

SOLDIER. And the Lord said...*(He waits for KAREN's answer.)* Have you forgotten? He said, "Let there be light, and there was light." *(He turns mockingly to the VILLAGERS.)* You see, I can quote scripture. *(Then to KAREN again.)* And then, Karen? *(KAREN is unable to answer. SOLDIER, silkily.)* You forget so soon how the world was created? Ah, Karen, you must have been thinking about something other than your lesson. *(Intently.)* What was it, Karen? What were you thinking about? *(KAREN looks up slowly, drawn to the OLD SOLDIER's eyes. ALL are breathlessly waiting her answer.)*

KAREN *(finally answering, as though in a trance)*. I was thinking about my red shoes. *(There is a murmur that subsides as the OLD SOLDIER goes on.)*

SOLDIER. What about your shoes, Karen?

KAREN. They are the most beautiful shoes in all the world, and they are mine!

SOLDIER. Vanity, vanity! Have you never heard that he who dancing shoes to church will wear, must dance forever and everywhere? *(He turns suddenly to the VILLAGERS.)* You were right! Red shoes are not to be worn to church! Not these red shoes! Ah, Karen, look at them. They are dusty. Let me dust them for you! *(He approaches KAREN, who still stands transfixed. He takes his pipe and begins to play "The Shoemaker's Dance." He bends down low and taps the shoes with a flourish. He dances a bit to his music, pointing the pipe constantly at the shoes. KAREN begins to respond, and dances haltingly, wonderingly, until at last she dances in the courtyard. The OLD SOLDIER continues to play, half following her about as her dance increases in momentum. Her trance-like state changes into one of joyous abandon.)*

KAREN. I'm dancing! My red shoes make me dance! Oh, my red shoes make me dance!

SOLDIER. Dance, Karen, dance! Who dancing shoes to church will wear, must dance forever and everywhere! *(He whirls off-stage. With the OLD SOLDIER gone—though his music continues—ALL on the stage are released from the spell of his presence and react to the dancing.)*

FRU NIELSEN. Karen!

GRANDMOTHER. What is she doing?

FRU SORENSEN. She is dancing!

SHOEMAKER. What has he done? *(She stares off-stage where the OLD SOLDIER had made his exit, beginning to realize that he is not what he appears to be.)*

FRU NIELSEN. Karen, stop!

RODHOLM. Stop, I say.

GRANDMOTHER. Karen! Karen! *(She stands stricken, and her thoughts fly back to the tragic time when she wore her red shoes.)*

NURSE. She is bewitched.

FRU NIELSEN. Or gone mad. *(KAREN dances to the CHILDREN and involves some of them in her dance by taking their hands and swinging them about. They scream and run away. She then dances defiantly toward the VILLAGERS, and slips out of each one's grasp. The church bells begin to ring. KAREN stops abruptly for a moment, and dances toward the church. It would appear that she would like to stop dancing, as though in response to the bells, but with slight movements of her feet, she dances backward away from the church.)*

KAREN *(realizing she cannot stop)*. I can't stop dancing! I can't stop!

GRANDMOTHER. Take off your shoes, Karen. Take them off! *(KAREN dances to the bench, C, and tries to take off her shoes.)*

KAREN. I can't get them off! My shoes won't come off! *(She is impelled to dance again and dances a wild whirling figure.)* I can't stop! My red shoes...help me...Oh my red shoes, oh my red shoes! *(As the VILLAGERS rush to stop her, she leaps on the bench, and as they close in on her, she leaps to the top of the wall, where she dances away from their outstretched arms. With a final whirl, she leaps off down the hill. The VILLAGERS and CHILDREN scream and they watch her dancing, out of our sight, down the hill as the music fades away. RODHOLM and the three BOYS run out the gate. Then, utter silence.)*

GRANDMOTHER *(apprehensively)*. What has happened? ...Karen?

NURSE. She danced to the top of the wall and leaped off down the hill.

GRANDMOTHER. Oh, Karen! You, too...you, too!

NURSE. She did not fall. She danced down the hill, unhurt.

INGE. How she danced!

MARTA. Down that steep hill!

FRU NIELSEN. Look, look! There she is, way down the road! You can see her red shoes twinkling in the sun!

(Those who had left the wall rush back again. Exclamations ad lib. As they watch, the BOYS and RODHOLM return, out of breath.)

RODHOLM *(marveling)*. She never once fell down that steep hill. She danced all the way.

HANS. Did she go!

OLUF. Nobody could catch her!

GRANDMOTHER. Nurse, quickly, to the carriage. We will follow her down the road. *(NURSE and GRANDMOTHER go out via the gate.)*

FRU NIELSEN *(vindictively)*. What does she expect? Allowing her to wear red shoes to church. *(Church bells resume ringing.)*

RODHOLM. Let us go in, and forget not to pray for her.

(ALL file into church, the last to go up the steps being the SHOEMAKER. She pauses to take one last look over the wall and sees the OLD SOLDIER entering DR, highly pleased with himself.)

SHOEMAKER. You! What have you done?!

SOLDIER. I? I have done nothing but furnish the leather for the red shoes.

SHOEMAKER *(coming down the steps)*. You made her dance, you...you...whatever you are.

SOLDIER. I only helped Karen get what she wanted. She wanted red shoes, so she got red shoes...like the Princess. She wanted to dance, so now she is dancing...like the Princess.

SHOEMAKER *(trying desperately to make the SOLDIER understand)*. But her shoes! She can't take them off! She can't stop dancing! What will happen to her?

SOLDIER. Is that any business of yours...Shoe...maker? *(His coldness shocks the SHOEMAKER, as does the peculiar emphasis he placed on the word "Shoe-maker," which implicates her in KAREN's fate. She involuntarily looks at her hands, and in growing realization of her part in the OLD SOLDIER's scheme, backs away from him in fear. He merely takes out his pipe and jauntily plays "The Shoemaker's Dance" as the curtain falls.)*

CURTAIN

END OF ACT TWO

ACT THREE

SETTING: *The same scene, early evening a week later.*

AT RISE: *HANS and OLUF are on the stage when the curtain opens, watching the road below the hill.*

HANS *(with suppressed excitement)*. There he comes!
OLUF. I knew he'd make it! Hi, Nils! We're here!
HANS. Ssshhh!

(They go to the gate, and in a moment, NILS appears.)

NILS. Here I am.
HANS. Did you have any trouble getting away?
NILS. Naw! I just ducked out the back door.
OLUF. Did you see any of the girls?
NILS. They won't come. They're too scared.
HANS. Well, the whole town is scared. Isn't it crazy? Just because a girl puts on red shoes and starts to dance, we can't do anything.
OLUF. My father says there's more to this than we know.
NILS. But how is anybody going to know more about it being locked up in their houses? Grown-ups! If I had my way...
HANS. Ssshhhhh! *(The BOYS listen attentively.)*
OLUF. Someone's coming!

(The BOYS duck down against the wall Left of the bench, watching the gate. INGE, THORA, and MARTA enter. They do not see the BOYS.)

INGE. They're not here.

THORA. They said this morning they'd be here.

MARTA. I wish I'd stayed home.

INGE. Scaredy-cat. *(The BOYS, who have been keeping each other quiet, take advantage of the opportunity, and jump up in grotesque poses as they yell "Boo!" The GIRLS scream and the BOYS laugh while the GIRLS recover from their fright.)*

HANS. Who's scaredy-cat now?

INGE. Oh, you...Scaring us like that! I could just...

HANS. Could just what. *(He is ready to enjoy a chase.)*

INGE. I know you. You'd just jump up on that wall again.

HANS. You could jump up after me.

MARTA. How can you talk like that? I can still see her dancing on top of the wall...before she jumped off...

HANS. Well, I wouldn't jump off. I haven't got on red shoes.

MARTA. Hans! Be still! That's all I've heard all week... red shoes, red shoes, red shoes...

THORA. That's all my mother keeps talking about, too. Karen and her red shoes.

OLUF. My father says that's all anybody talks about.

INGE. Well, we came here so we could get away from all that. Cooped up all week in the house. Don't do this, don't do that, don't go outside or the Old Soldier will get you...

MARTA. Be quiet!...Besides, it wasn't the Old Soldier. It was the Shoemaker. She made the shoes.

INGE. But you saw how the Old Soldier played his pipe and made her dance!

THORA. What's the difference? Old Soldier, Shoemaker, we can't go out to play as long as they're around. Come on, what shall we play?

HANS. Tag. You're it! *(He tags INGE and runs away, stopping in an attitude that clearly indicates he will jump on the wall if chased.)*

INGE. I don't feel like playing tag.

MARTA. I don't, either. *(To THORA.)* Did you bring your jacks?

THORA. No.

NILS *(in disgust)*. Girls' games. *(He wanders to the wall UL. The other CHILDREN sit or loll about, clearly not knowing what to do with their liberty. NILS looks out over the wall.)* I wonder where she is now?

INGE. I don't know and I don't care.

MARTA. Inge, how can you say that!

INGE. Well, if it wasn't for her, we wouldn't be kept inside all the time. As though we'd put on red shoes and dance away someplace.

MARTA *(shocked)*. Inge!

INGE. It's true, isn't it? But she got just what she had coming to her, lying about her shoes being black, and thinking about her shoes in church...

OLUF. She tried to steal the Princess' shoes, too.

MARTA. You don't know that for sure.

INGE. And putting on her uppity airs after Grandmother Nissen took her in.

MARTA. I think you're horrid. We should feel sorry for her.

THORA. Sorry!

MARTA. She wasn't to blame. It was that old Shoemaker. She's a witch, that's what she is!

HANS *(incredibly)*. Witch! You believe in witches?

MARTA. Well...I never did believe in them. But I think the Shoemaker is a...

(The SHOEMAKER has pushed her cart on the stage from DL. In addition to the shoes, the cart now has on it some bundles of clothes.)

SHOEMAKER *(harshly)*. Well, the Shoemaker is a what? *(As the CHILDREN do not answer.)* Speak up! *(The CHILDREN remain silent, backing away from her.)* Look, children. I made your shoes, everyone of them. You can take them off at night, can't you? Go up on the wall and jump off. Your shoes won't save you from falling down the hill. I just make shoes—ordinary shoes that...*(She stops as she realizes the futility of trying to explain. Then, dully.)* Have you seen the Old Soldier? *(The CHILDREN shake their heads.)*

HANS. We haven't seen him. We haven't been allowed to go out.

SHOEMAKER. So I hear. This whole village is afraid of its own shadows. But you—you children. *(Pleading.)* You must not believe in the terrible things they say about me. I am not to blame for what happened to Karen. Do you hear? I was not to blame. *(As the CHILDREN back away from her, frightened.)* See my shoes? *(She takes some shoes from her cart.)* Good shoes they are, like your own, and they won't make anyone dance. See them? See them? *(She becomes vehement and approaches the CHILDREN, who scatter and run off. She shouts after them.)* They won't make you dance! Here! Try them!

(The SHOEMAKER throws the shoes after the CHILDREN, slumps, and goes back wearily to her cart, against which she leans, trying to collect her thoughts. GRANDMOTHER and the NURSE enter through the gate.)

GRANDMOTHER *(eagerly)*. And is Karen here?

NURSE. No, Grandmother, she is not.

GRANDMOTHER. Surely I thought I might find her here.

NURSE. There is only the Shoemaker.

GRANDMOTHER. Shoemaker? *(Coming forward eagerly.)* Shoemaker, are you here?

SHOEMAKER. Yes.

GRANDMOTHER. Have you seen Karen?

SHOEMAKER *(bitterly)*. Karen? Karen be cursed!

GRANDMOTHER *(shocked at her bitterness)*. Shoemaker!

SHOEMAKER. That cursed girl and her red shoes!

GRANDMOTHER *(gently)*. Why so bitter?

SHOEMAKER *(seizing several shoes from her cart)*. All my life I have been selling shoes in this countryside and village. Comes this ragamuffin and her red shoes, and no one buys shoes from me anymore. Shoes, they say? And how do I know I will not dance off among the hills if I buy your shoes? So the doors are slammed in my face, and the dogs are turned loose upon me, for the fear of the red shoes has traveled from house to house like the plague, as if all my shoes are infected. *(She puts the shoes back on her cart.)*

GRANDMOTHER. My poor woman. I should not have bought those shoes from you.

NURSE. Oh, Grandmother, when will you stop whipping yourself with remorse! It was not your fault that Karen bought red shoes. You couldn't see their color...

GRANDMOTHER. That's just it, Nurse. I couldn't see their color. They looked shiny, so I thought they were black. I should have made sure.

NURSE. But, Grandmother...

GRANDMOTHER. No, Nurse! One who is responsible must be able to see. I made myself responsible for Karen without seeing what I was doing.

NURSE. Then I am guilty, too. I should have told you her shoes were red.

GRANDMOTHER. I think you tried to tell me, didn't you?

NURSE. I should have insisted on telling you. I could see, but I thought it was none of my business.

GRANDMOTHER. It wasn't.

NURSE. No, Grandmother. It *was* my business to tell you.

GRANDMOTHER. It is too easy a way out to say, "You should have told me." Why, I could as easily say that the Princess is to blame, because if she had not asked me to give Karen a home, I would not have bought her red shoes...Or to say the Shoemaker is to blame, for she could have told me. The fault is mine, Nurse, and it lies heavily on my heart, and nothing you say takes away one bit of its weight. *(GRANDMOTHER presses her handkerchief to her eyes and turns away. The NURSE looks at her compassionately and then turns to the SHOEMAKER.)*

NURSE. This is the way she has been all week. She has given herself no rest, driving up and down the countryside, trying to find Karen.

SHOEMAKER. That cursed girl with her fancy dreams of wearing red shoes.

NURSE. I wish I could think of some way to help her. *(Thinks a moment.)* How did you happen to have those shoes?

SHOEMAKER. I made them, like I make all my shoes.

NURSE. They were made of beautiful leather.

SHOEMAKER *(remembering)*. Aye, they were. The most beautiful leather I ever worked upon. When I cut the pieces to make the shoes, my shears seemed to work themselves. And my needle never stitched a finer seam, or as fast, as when I made the red shoes.

NURSE. Where did you get the leather?

SHOEMAKER. I got the leather because I lost a wager with the Old Soldier.

NURSE. How can that be, to get something because you *lose* a wager.

SHOEMAKER. If I had won, the leather would have been mine.

NURSE. You mean, win or lose, the leather would have been yours? *(Obviously puzzled.)*

SHOEMAKER. No, I lost the wager, so I got to *use* the leather to make the pair of shoes. If I had won, I would have just gotten the leather, see?

NURSE. But surely, if you would have won the leather, you would have made the shoes, too.

SHOEMAKER. Of course! But with this difference. The shoes would have been mine to sell, then.

GRANDMOTHER *(who had been drawn to the conversation and following it closely).* But you sold me the shoes.

SHOEMAKER *(realizing for the first time).* Yes...I did! And they weren't mine to sell, really. Those shoes belonged to the Old Soldier! But when that girl picked them out, I just...sold them, anyway.

NURSE *(reprovingly).* You should not have sold what was not yours to sell. *(To GRANDMOTHER.)* There now, Grandmother, she is to blame for what happened to Karen.

GRANDMOTHER. She is not to blame. She is in the business of making and selling shoes.

SHOEMAKER. Yes, but I have sold no shoes since Karen picked the red ones. *(She returns to her former mood.)* I see them on Karen's feet, dancing down the hill and away. I try to sleep at night, and I see Karen in her red shoes, dancing among the cornstalks in the fields, flitting like a ghost with red feet in the dark forests. When I do fall asleep, I wake up with a start, because I think I see Karen dancing in the lonely place where the Executioner dwells.

GRANDMOTHER *(comfortingly).* Bad dreams, bad dreams.

SHOEMAKER. Sometimes I think all that has happened is a dream. But when people shrink from me and buy no shoes, then I *know* there is a Karen, that there *are* red shoes, and that *I* made them. And now I also know that win or lose my wager with the old soldier, I would have made those shoes because he wanted me to make them.

NURSE. Where is the Old Soldier?

SHOEMAKER. I have not seen him. And I don't want to see him, because if it were not for him, I would not be sneaking off like a thief, to sell shoes in another town. *(She considers that for a moment.)* I am almost fearful of selling another pair of shoes. *(With bitter humor.)* Maybe I should not sell shoes anymore, but sell crutches to those who cannot walk. *(She begins to go Left, pushing her cart.)*

GRANDMOTHER *(shakes her head sadly, then calls to the SHOEMAKER)*. Shoemaker, if you should see or hear of Karen in your travels...

SHOEMAKER. If I should see or hear of her, I'll curse her roundly. *(She goes out with her cart.)*

GRANDMOTHER *(after a pause)*. So bitter, poor woman.

NURSE. Well, Grandmother, what now?

GRANDMOTHER. I do not know. I only know there is no rest, no peace for me until Karen stops dancing. *(She takes a few steps away, helplessly. She peers at the church looming in the evening shadows, and walks toward it, looking up as though seeing its spire.)* Come here, Nurse. This is the church of my childhood. When I was a baby in my mother's arms, I was baptized here. My mother took me to church here every Sunday, and when she died, she was buried from this church. My mother taught me that, when all hope and refuge was gone, not to forget to turn to the dwelling place of the Lord...Help me up the steps. *(They go up, and she turns at the door.)* I will go in...alone.

NURSE. You do not want me to stay with you?

GRANDMOTHER. No. Let me be alone. *(Reassuringly.)* I will not stumble. Wait for me in the carriage, for I will be here for some time.

(GRANDMOTHER goes into the church. The NURSE watches her go, closes the door softly, and goes out through the gate. After a moment, "The Shoemaker's Dance" music is heard softly. KAREN enters L, led by the EXECUTIONER, who is dressed as the OLD SOLDIER had described him. KAREN is dancing wearily and never stops throughout the scene. Her steps are slow, with just enough movement of the feet to indicate dancing. From time to time, she breaks into a figure as suggested by her lines. See Production Notes.)

EXECUTIONER. Is this the place?

KAREN. This is the place. This is where I started dancing.

EXECUTIONER. Don't you think you ought to stop?

KAREN. Stop? I have tried to stop, but I can't. Oh, I am so weary! *(She throws herself on the bench, C, and tries to take off her shoes. Again she is impelled to dance.)* Oh, can't you help me?

EXECUTIONER. Whatever help I could give would be of a sort most people do not want. Remember, I am the executioner.

KAREN. Oh, no, no! Without my head I could not repent. I could no longer be sorry for what I did. No, I must dance on. *(She sweeps into a dance for a few moments.)* Only there is no longer any music. I heard music—once. When I danced down the hill...but I hear no music now. *(She dances again.)*

EXECUTIONER *(shaking his head in pity)*. I must leave you, strange girl.

KAREN. Oh, no! Stay! You have been kind to me! You are my only friend.

EXECUTIONER. I, a kind friend? I am the executioner. People fear me, and I must live in the lonely place among the bones of those whose lives I have taken.

KAREN. Yes, you are my friend. Please don't leave me.

EXECUTIONER. As a friend, I will stay.

KAREN. See, this is where it all started. *(Dancing a figure as suggested by her lines.)* I went into the church—with my red shoes. When I walked down the aisle, I saw all the pictures of the saints looking at my shoes. I was so proud! They nodded their heads as though to say, "See Karen and her red shoes. There are no other shoes like them in all the world." And when I came out of the church, my red shoes shone in the sun, and I heard music that turned me into a Princess, and everybody was at my command! I wanted to dance, and dance I did...but now I am so weary, and so sorry that I thought of nothing but my red shoes when I was in church.

EXECUTIONER. When one is in church, one's thoughts should be with God.

KAREN. I know that now. I was wrong...oh so wrong. I tried to steal shoes, too. And I lied about my shoes and said they were black. Can't I be forgiven?

EXECUTIONER. *I* forgive you, if that is any help.

KAREN. Oh, you are a friend, to forgive me! If I could only stop dancing then I know I would be forgiven. Oh, how I have danced! Down the hill and over the fields, where the corn grows, and into the deep, dark wood. The sun beat down upon me, and at night the moon shone. See, the red moon is coming up behind the trees. It is round, and red, as red as...oh!

(KAREN gasps and points toward the gate, where a red glow fades up, to reveal the OLD SOLDIER. He steps into the courtyard.)

KAREN. Oh, Old Soldier, make me stop dancing!

SOLDIER. No, Karen, you will dance until the leaves of the trees fall from the branches. You will dance from house to house and knock on the doors of all vain proud children. You wanted to dance, so dance you must, until your bones have turned to dust.

EXECUTIONER. He made you dance? *(He faces up to the OLD SOLDIER.)*

KAREN. Yes, yes, he did. Ask him, plead with him for me, so I may stop dancing.

EXECUTIONER. He will pay no heed to me. I know him.

KAREN. You know him?

EXECUTIONER. Do you see this axe, Karen? He gave it to me, and I took it because he promised me great wealth. I am wealthy—I get a thousand crowns whenever I execute a hapless victim—but I have found no way to get rid of this axe. And, until I do, I shall have no friends.

KAREN *(wonderingly)*. You cannot drop your axe?

EXECUTIONER. Even as you cannot take off your shoes, I cannot rid myself of this axe.

KAREN *(despairingly)*. Then I must dance forever? *(KAREN and the EXECUTIONER are a forlorn twosome, as the OLD SOLDIER stands implacably before them.)*

EXECUTIONER *(sadly)*. The old soldier never relents. *(The axe in his hand gives him an idea.)* I can help you in one way only.

KAREN. Then help me!

EXECUTIONER. Kneel down, and I will cut off your dancing feet.

SOLDIER. That would please me, too, for then I could have my shoes again. But she won't do it. Karen wants to dance!

(The SHOEMAKER enters from DR with her cart piled high with crutches.)

SHOEMAKER. Crutches? Crutches? Who will buy crutches? *(Taking crutches from cart which she leaves DR. The scene is played with an air of unreality, like a dream.)*

SOLDIER. We have no need for crutches. Karen wants to dance!

SHOEMAKER *(offering crutches)*. Crutches! Crutches!

SOLDIER *(pointing at her shoes)*. Dance! Dance!

EXECUTIONER (at the church steps). Kneel! Kneel! *(The above is chanted over and over again. KAREN looks wildly from one to the other as they repeat their chants.)*

KAREN. I will do it! I will stop dancing so I can live to repent! *(She runs to the church steps and kneels.)* Hurry, and be merciful!

EXECUTIONER. I shall be quick.

(The EXECUTIONER is DL of the church steps. As he raises his axe, the church doors open slowly and light begins to stream from inside the church. We hear the VOICE of an ANGEL, singing. KAREN remains kneeling, her head bowed in her hands. The OTHERS back away in awe, the OLD SOLDIER cowering at the gate, his arms over his eyes. The light from the church be-

comes brighter as the song of the ANGEL grows in volume. See Production Notes.)

ANGEL *(singing).*

Karen, Karen, hear me,
The help you seek is near thee,
Raise thy head and lift thine eyes
To angels come from Paradise,
Karen, Karen, hear me.

(The ANGEL appears at the door, and as she sings the second verse, she is joined by the SECOND ANGEL from within the church, who sings a descant.)

ANGELS *(singing).*

Karen, Karen, hear me,
Repentance has become thee,
For even as you kneel to pray,
Forgiven is your errant way,
Karen, Karen, hear me.

(The SECOND ANGEL appears at the door. The two ANGELS kneel at KAREN's feet as they sing the third verse and remove the red shoes. They lift her gently to her feet, and lead her into the church as their music and the brilliant light fade away. They take the red shoes with them. During the scene, the SHOEMAKER unobtrusively gets rid of her cart and crutches.)

ANGELS *(singing).*

Karen, Karen, hear me,
The help you seek is near thee.
Have no fear and have no dread,

You'll dance no more in shoes of red,
Karen, Karen, hear me.

(If necessary, the ANGELS may hum their song to cover their business and exit.)

SOLDIER *(springing to life as he uncovers his eyes)*. The red shoes! Where are the red shoes?! *(The SHOEMAKER points silently toward the church. Vehemently.)* They are my shoes. My red shoes! *(He runs toward the church as though to rescue them, but checks himself at the steps. He glares helplessly at the EXECUTIONER, then at the SHOEMAKER.)* I will not have those shoes taken from me! *(Wheedling, to the EXECUTIONER.)* Get them for me...

EXECUTIONER. Not I. You haven't enough in your kingdom to tempt me again.

SOLDIER. Then you, Shoemaker. Get them for me and I will keep you in leather for the rest of your life.

SHOEMAKER. No, no! *(Backing away from him DR.)* I don't trust you. No!

SOLDIER *(flaring up in anger)*. I must have those shoes! *(He makes a violent gesture and he sees the pipe in his hand. Craftily, he looks at the EXECUTIONER, then at the SHOEMAKER.)* So you think you'll keep me from my shoes, eh? I'll show them to you, Shoemaker, there on the steps. Watch! *(He places the pipe between his lips and, pointing it toward the church steps, he begins to play, much as he did when he caused KAREN to dance. He plays intently, building up the suspense, until presently the red shoes are dancing in the church doorway. See Production Notes.)*

SHOEMAKER *(in awe)*. The red shoes! They are dancing out of the church!

SOLDIER *(triumphantly)*. See, Shoemaker? There are the shoes! Shoes that will never wear out! Look at them—pick them up—you'll see they are as new as when you made them! *(Softly, temptingly.)* Look at them, Shoemaker, look at the red shoes; look at them. *(As the OLD SOLDIER repeats his lines, the SHOEMAKER looks unbelievingly at the OLD SOLDIER, and moves slowly toward the shoes as though to pick them up. The OLD SOLDIER watches her intently, greedily, for he knows this is his only chance to retrieve the shoes. He keeps urging her on, and as the SHOEMAKER pauses at C, he gets behind her and plays his pipe. She falters forward, and as she nears the steps, her hands outstretched to seize the shoes, the EXECUTIONER springs forward.)*

EXECUTIONER. Don't touch those shoes, you fool! Don't you know who he is? *(The EXECUTIONER pushes the SHOEMAKER violently to one side, and frantically brings his axe down on the shoes, but keeps missing them. He raises his axe high in a last supreme effort, and the axe clatters from his hands and falls to the church steps. He looks at his hands, throws back his hood over his shoulders, and tears the mask off his eyes, a free man, and recedes into the shadows DL. The OLD SOLDIER lunges desperately forward to seize the shoes and is bathed in the brilliant light from the church. The shoes are just out of his grasp and as the VOICES of the ANGELS sing, he cringes and twists away, bathed in a red light, stealing a last desperate look at the red shoes shining in the white light in the church doorway, as the curtain falls.)*

CURTAIN—END OF PLAY

PRODUCTION NOTES

SETTING: The play takes place in a village in Denmark in the 1870's. The period is not arbitrary, but has been selected because it was the time of Hans Christian Andersen, and his story seems to reflect the mores of his times.

The scene is a courtyard in front of a quaint old rustic church on top of a hill. The church is UL with three steps leading to its double doors. The opening into the church should be plainly visible to the audience because of important action that takes place there.

The courtyard is enclosed by a stone wall that runs across the back of the stage, and diagonally on the Right. A wrought iron gate is UR. This exit leads to steps down the hill, and if the stage has a trap door, these can be practical steps. Otherwise, the steps can be masked by shrubbery, and the ascent and descent can be indicated by the actors looking down an imaginary stairway. The steps lead to an imaginary road that curves around the base of the hill.

The background is of sky, with perhaps treetops in the distance. A large tree that shades the courtyard is DR, with a rustic bench around its ancient trunk. Another bench is UC. There are entrances DR and DL as though to a narrow street, leading to two parts of the village.

COSTUMES: It is important that the costume designer eliminate the use of the color red in costuming the PRINCESS, the Lady, KAREN in Act II, and the CHILDREN and VILLAGERS who enter the church. The color is used symbolically in the play, and the point of not wearing red shoes to church (because they are the color of the devil, as FRU NIELSEN says) is lost if other actors wear red ribbons, hose, or accessories. In other words, red is simply not worn to church.

In Act II, it is suggested that the WOMEN wear black dresses, relieved with white. The CHILDREN could also wear white. KAREN's Act II costume could also be white, accenting the red shoes. A duplicate costume should be made for Act III, and made ragged and smudged as it would be after a week of dancing in the countryside. Peasant-type costumes, either authentic or imaginative, should be used for Act I.

MUSIC: The music throughout the play is an important and integral part of the production. Because production facilities, budgets, and talent vary widely, there are a number of alternatives presented herewith to meet varying conditions.

I. The OLD SOLDIER may synchronize his playing with an off-stage musician. Instruments suggested are the clarinet, flute, oboe, recorder, piccolo, and the violin. KAREN's dance may be played by the same musician, solo or accompanied on the piano, playing "THE SHOEMAKER'S DANCE."

II. The OLD SOLDIER, if played by a skilled-enough musician, may play his own music on the stage, with instruments as suggested above.

III. It is possible to have all the music, including the OLD SOLDIER's, played off-stage by a piano, although this would not be as effective as a wind instrument. In this case, the OLD SOLDIER could play a small guitar, in keeping with the sound of strings.

IV. A combination of any of the above is possible: for example, a live off-stage musician to play the OLD SOLDIER's piping, the record for KAREN's dance, ANGELS actually singing. In any event, incorporate the music into the rehearsals at an early date to achieve smoothness and good synchronization.

The musician's pipe played by the OLD SOLDIER can be a small recorder, a miniature clarinet purchased at a variety store, a shepherd's pipe of bamboo, small flute, etc. This "fake" instrument need not be of regular size; indeed, the smaller size is easier to handle on the stage. Whatever is used, it should look real, and typical of the period.

The singing of the ANGELS is best done by the actors playing the parts. If they are not skilled enough, it is not effective if they fake singing with the off-stage music. Have them do their entrances and business as described while the music is sung off.

Melody lines for the music used in the play can be found in the back of this book. You may make your own piano accompaniment or orchestration. All the melodies are in the public domain and are authentic Danish folk tunes, except for the "SONG OF THE ANGELS," which is original. You may also wish to substitute music of your own choice.

DANCES: Like the music, the dances in the play are an integral part of the production, because the story of the red shoes is a story of dancing shoes. KAREN's dance, therefore, is worthy of the best that can be created by your production staff.

However, KAREN's dance need not be a full-fledged ballet. A girl with natural rhythm and grace can freely interpret the dance as described. If a girl trained in interpretive or ballet dancing is available, so much the better. However, if a choice must be made between a talented dancer who cannot act too well, and a more talented actor who can dance freely, the latter is the better choice. KAREN's role is an actor's, not a dancer's.

If the actors who play the OLD SOLDIER and the EXECUTIONER can dance (either freely or as trained), it is possible to have them dance with KAREN in their respective scenes.

Lastly, it is possible, if you have enough trained dancers as your actors, to create a short ballet from the scene where KAREN dances, utilizing KAREN, The OLD SOLDIER, some of the CHILDREN, and the VILLAGERS.

These dances open up many possibilities, from the simple to the complex. Be sure to rehearse them adequately and to make them a part of a smooth-flowing production.

The folk dances do not present any difficulties. They are danced as follows:

SHOEMAKER'S DANCE

Formation: Partners facing each other. Raise closed fists chest high and revolve them around each other rapidly, measure 1.

Reverse the direction of revolving, measure 2.

Push elbows backward twice as though pulling a thread between the closed fists, in time with music, measure 3.

Open left fist and rap right fist down sharply three times, in time with music, measure 4.

Measures 1 to 4 are repeated with the same figure.

Partners quickly form a single circle, in file formation, not holding hands, and skip forward counterclockwise as measures 5 to 8 are repeated twice. They then form into partners facing again and repeat the dance.

The dance describes a shoemaker at work, winding his bobbin, waxing his thread, and pounding pegs (nails) into the shoe. The second half describes the customer going home from the shop with his shoes. Words may be sung by the dancers.

Wind, wind, wind the bobbin,
Wind, wind, wind the bobbin,
Pull, pull, pound in pegs (repeat).
Stitch them up and stitch them down,
I've got the finest shoes in town (repeat).

THE SEVEN JUMPS

Formation: Children in a single circle, holding hands, no partners.

Skip to the left, measures 1 and 2.

Skip to the right, measures 3 and 4.

1. Hold up one leg, stork fashion, for the duration of the long note, down on floor on short note.

2. The skipping to the left, and to the right is repeated, and the right foot is held up, stork fashion, according to the length of the long note, then the right foot similarly.

The dance is repeated, and each time the musician adds another long and short note (varying the length of the notes each time), with the following actions.

3. Kneel on right knee.

4. Kneel on left knee.

5. Bend forward (kneeling) right elbow on floor, chin in hand.

6. As above, left elbow as well as the right on floor, chin in hand.

7. Forehead on floor.

The musician also may delay the beginning of the "skipping" music, and dancers hold whatever "jump" they may be doing until the music indicates they are to skip.

It is suggested that the dance be danced completely, and that KAREN say her lines, "She's here, she's here" as the CHILDREN are resting their heads on the floor for the 7th jump, or as they are completing the dance with a final skipping around after the 7th jump. She will have to "top" the sound of the music and dancing in order to be heard.

ROSALILLE

The music should fade in on the chorus of "Ha, ha, ha, sa-sa, sa-sa," to give the PRINCESS time to listen and hold the LADY's hand. They will then be in a position to dance as the verse begins.

Formation: Holding hands, facing front. Count 1-2-3, starting to count with 3-and. Each count of the first 12 measures represents a step as follows:

3-and, step to the left/ 1, step with right foot behind left foot/

2, step to the left with the left foot/ 3, bring right foot across the front of the left pointing the toe/ 1, step to the right with the right/ 2, step with the left foot behind the right/

3, step to the right with the right/ 1, bring left foot across the right and point the toe, and repeat for the first 12 measures.

On "Ha, ha, ha, ha," partners bow and curtsy to each other.

On "Sa-sa, sa-sa," partners bow and curtsy slightly away from each other.

The two bows and curtsies are repeated.

Partners join hands, swing them up and take a step forward on "laughed," swing hands down and take a step forward on "jested," and repeat on "merry" and "they."

The last figure need not be repeated the second time though, for the singer's voice should fade off by that time.

SCENERY AND LIGHTING: The scenery does not present any unusual problems. Keep it simple and rustic. It should tend to create the feeling of being on top of a hill. The church spire does not need to be shown, as it can be masked by foliage borders. On low ceilinged stages, just the lower part of the church can be shown.

For authenticity, consult pictures of old churches that exist in Vossevangen, Norway, one of which is actually situated on a hill.

KAREN will need a sturdy platform behind the wall on which to dance. This platform should not be attached to the scenery proper. There is too much danger of having the wall vibrate as she dances. Even a table may be placed behind the wall for her to dance on. The height of the table should be just an inch or so below the height of the wall. HANS uses the same platform or table for his wall-walking in the first scene.

Room must be provided for the SHOEMAKER's cart off-stage, sufficient to allow it to be turned around. This occurs twice in the play: once when the SHOEMAKER makes the shoes, and once when she returns on the stage with the crutches. If the latter presents an insurmountable difficulty, due to lack of space, the SHOEMAKER may enter carrying the crutches in her hands.

To create the illusion of the OLD SOLDIER rising with the moon, he should hide between the wall and the woodwings masking the UR exit. When the lights come up—a spotlight UR will be most effective—he stands from a squatting position. This is more effective than if he enters from the "steps" and through the gate.

To counteract sharp shadows on the ANGELS made by the light from within the church, a spotlight should be prefocused on them from the borders UR of Center.

THE DANCING SHOES: It is best to use an extra pair of shoes which have been fitted out with the manipulating device of your choice. There are several ways to manipulate the shoes.

I. Marionette style. Connect the heels and toes of the shoes to three strings, one at the toe, two at the sides of the heel, to give it balance. A manipulator's bridge is built above the door of the church. The shoes are at the right and left of the doors, unseen by the audience. On cue, "dance" the shoes from their positions to the center of the doorway. The shoes may also dance from one side of the doors.

II. Rod-Puppet style. Shoes are placed as above—to one side, or to either side of the door—each shoe connected to a rod of stiff wire. The wire extends below the platform floor through a slit in the floor. Operators lie below the floor and manipulate the rods to "dance" the shoes.

By changing the direction of the bridge or the slit in the floor, the shoes can be made to dance in a line at right angles to the door, as though dancing from a center aisle.

III. Rod-and-string. This method is for a "long-distance" control in which the shoes would appear to be coming from the center aisle. A sufficient length of 1" x 1/4" clear pine lathing is used to push the shoes from where the hidden operator stands in the wings to the doorway of the church. The lathing should be painted the same color as the floor of the platform, preferably black.

At the shoe end of the lath, fasten a 7" length of stiff wire crosswise to the lath. The toes of the shoes are hinged to the wire, sewn, or glued with cloth. Another stiff wire, 13" long, is fastened to the lath about 1" behind the heels of the shoes, the lath centered on the wire. 4" of the wire is then bent up on both ends and a small eyelet soldered to the ends of the upright wires. Black nylon cord, heavy thread, or lightweight black fish line is fastened to the bottom of the heels of the shoes, up through the eyelet, and through two screw eyes about 4" behind the heels, and thus to the operator. Pushing the lath forward with a slight rotary motion and pulling and releasing the strings will "dance" the shoes. All hardware and parts must be black.

-THE RED SHOES-

"SONG OF THE ANGELS"

Karl J. Schmidt

"SHOEMAKER'S CHANT"

"SHOEMAKER'S DANCE"

"SEVEN JUMPS"

"ROSALILLE"

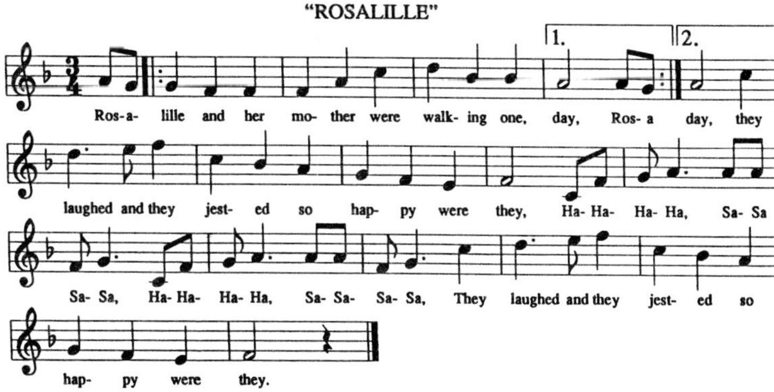

DIRECTOR'S NOTES

DIRECTOR'S NOTES

DIRECTOR'S NOTES

DIRECTOR'S NOTES

DIRECTOR'S NOTES